C000076061

NOBLE ART

TOM SAWYER

***An Artistic & Literary Celebration
of the Old English Prize-Ring.***

NOBLE ART

TOM SAWYER

UNWIN

HYMAN

LONDON SYDNEY WELLINGTON

First published in Great Britain by the Trade Division of
Unwin Hyman Limited, 1989.

Copyright ©1989 by Tom Sawyer

Designed by Tom Sawyer

All rights reserved. No part of this publication may be reproduced,
stored in a retrieval system, or transmitted in any form or by any means,
electronic, mechanical, photocopying, recording or otherwise,
without the prior permission of Unwin Hyman Limited.

UNWIN HYMAN LIMITED
15–17 Broadwick Street
London W1V 1FP

Allen & Unwin Australia Pty Ltd
8 Napier Street, North Sydney, NSW 2060, Australia

Allen & Unwin New Zealand Pty Ltd with the Port Nicholson Press
Compusales Building, 75 Ghuznee Street, Wellington, New Zealand

British Library Cataloguing in Publication Data
Sawyer, Tom
    Noble art: an artistic & literary celebration of the old English prize – ring.
    1. English literature. Special subjects. Prize fighting. Anthologies
    2. English graphic arts. Special subjects. Prize fighting
    I. Title
    820.8′0355

    ISBN 0-04-440351-8

Photoset in 11/12 Baskerville by Nene Phototypesetters Ltd, Northampton
Printed in Great Britain by Butler & Tanner Ltd, Frome

Frontispiece:
*'The Boxer's Arms, dedicated to the
Pugilistic Club, to Amateurs & the
Fancy in general' by George
Cruikshank. The figure emblazoned
on the 'sinister chief' in the act of
uncorking a bottle, is described in
punning terms worthy of Egan, as 'a
knight of the first drawing Claret'.*

CONTENTS

ACKNOWLEDGEMENTS

I would like to thank my old friend Nick Pallot for his expertise in correcting my dyslexic spelling and eccentric punctuation. My thanks are also due to Christine Bumstead for her patience in deciphering and typing the manuscript.

I am indebted to the library staff of Maidstone College of Art and Design, for their diligence in obtaining rare pugilistic material from other libraries, and to the collectors who have kindly loaned many of the illustrations reproduced in the following pages.

Bill Neill-Hall of Unwin Hyman has offered encouragement and made useful suggestions throughout; however, any remaining errors are entirely my own.

To my late father I owe a great debt of gratitude for instilling in me an interest in 'the sweet science' and the value of a good straight left. Finally, I am grateful to Jill for her tolerance of the pugilistic ephemera with which our house remains inundated.

DEDICATION

To the three great Toms, Cribb, Spring and Sayers, who with their brother pugilists were the inspiration for so much Noble Art.

Wood engraving from Pugilistica.

PREFACE

Most of us at some time during our lives have stood within the bar or lounge of an old-fashioned pub and gazed abstractedly at the walnut-framed sporting prints with which the walls of such establishments are often adorned. The pictures are usually of bygone hunting or racing scenes, but among them can occasionally be found a dusty, full-length portrait of 'Dutch Sam', 'Hammer Lane' or some other picturesquely named old English bruiser.

Stiffly posed and drawn with that charming naivety which so often characterises sporting art from the days before photography showed us how boxers really stood or horses really ran, they stare back defiantly at us from another age. Beneath the bruiser's portrait is sometimes displayed a list of battles fought, with details of numerous rounds and amounts of stake-money won or lost.

These pictures, which bear witness to a vanished England, where men fought sixty or seventy bare-knuckle rounds for the gratification of top-hatted bucks, will perhaps evoke the dim memory of a story by Hazlitt or George Borrow, a tale of the ring set in the 'good old days' of the Prince Regent or 'Butcher' Cumberland, when alternative entertainment was offered by bull-baiting, dog-fighting or a public execution.

The 150 years between 1720 and 1870 saw the rise, climax, decline and extinction of a social phenomenon which at its zenith reached vast proportions and came to be called 'Boximania'. This peculiarly English spectacle, which had its roots in the cudgelling booths of Stuart London, soon came to embrace all stratas of society, from the lowly costermonger up through the ranks of shopkeepers and businessmen to the highest in the land. At the same time as appealing to the baser instincts of the uneducated masses, it is to be expected that such a violent activity, when endowed with all the colourful trappings of chivalry, would also claim the attention of fashionable young men, with more money and leisure than sense. What at first comes as something of a shock, is the enthusiasm displayed for such a brutal spectacle by so many artists, poets and writers.

The painters Hogarth and Moreland were on friendly terms with prize-fighters, whilst the caricaturists Rowlandson and Gillray were often to be seen at ringside. Prize-fighting was

'Bendigo', an aquatint by Charles Hunt, published in 1846 as a companion to Hunt's earlier engraving of 'Deaf' Burke. It will be noticed that the 'southpaw' Bendigo leads with his right side, allowing the artist to portray him facing the portrait of the 'orthodox' Burke.
REPRODUCED BY COURTESY OF T. TULLEY.

described and prize-ring jargon used by many of the leading literary figures of the time, writers as respected and respectable as Fielding, Dickens and Thackeray. Lord Byron revelled in the company of pugilists, and poor diminutive John Clare, the shepherd poet, in his periods of insanity imagined himself to be a champion bruiser. Pugilism also produced writers like Pierce Egan and Vincent Dowling, who spent the greater part of their working lives specifically chronicling the events of the ring and the character of its protagonists. At the same time, literally tons of cheap prints and broadsheets were produced, depicting the latest heroes and most important fights, for the consumption of the illiterate or semi-literate masses.

The leading fighters were presented with ornate championship belts, silver cups and services of plate, by an admiring public. Eulogised and fêted by the literati and worshipped by the mob during their lifetime, in death they were commemorated with splendid tombs.

At the height of the craze for pugilism, the popular *Blackwood's Magazine* had remarked, albeit tongue in cheek, that 'the man who has not read *Boxiana* is ignorant of the power of the English language'. Moreover, prize-fighting as a popular spectacle was responsible for the introduction into our native tongue not just of slang words like 'claret', meaning blood, but of many metaphors still in common use. The phrase 'throw your hat into the ring', 'come up to scratch' and 'throw in the sponge', are all echoes of archaic prize-ring practice.

Pugilistic lore is preserved in the riotous antics of the cartoon characters Tom and Jerry, who were originally portrayed in human form as a pair of unruly Regency bucks, the invention of fight-reporter Pierce Egan.

The degree to which the memory of pugilism and pugilists has survived in popular culture may be gauged by the astounding quantity of folklore and legend surrounding the name of just one fighter. Besides being commemorated by an impressive stone lion which still guards his final resting place, William Thompson of Nottingham, who after twenty-eight sojourns in the 'house of correction' turned to religion, is celebrated in countless songs and ballads speedily produced by anonymous Victorian printers. He is also the subject of half a dozen or so 'autobiographies', the hero of a modern musical and the inspiration for some amusing broadsheet-style verses by Conan Doyle. The subject of many crudely produced sporting prints, Thompson also sat to a fashionable artist for his portrait in oils. The ring-name by which this roughneck bruiser was best known has since been appropriated by a brand of bottled beer, a public house in his native city, a highly successful racehorse, two annual races and an Australian Cathedral city, complete with its own resoundingly titled prelate 'The Rt Rev Bishop of Bendigo'.

This book is a celebration of the cultural survivals from a

bygone way of life. Set in the Georgian and Victorian eras, the participants should be seen and judged against a background of harsh social conditions, which, it is to be hoped, have vanished forever. The extraordinary fact remains that the appearance of two men, stripped to the waist, facing each other in a posture of defence within a roped enclosure, could and did provide the inspiration for so much art and literature. The pictorial and literary manifestations of the old English prize-ring, are, with the possible exception of cricket, the most extensive and varied of any sport – they are certainly by far the most exciting.

Broughton's Rules of 1743, an early-nineteenth-century broadsheet, decorated with wood engravings. Broughton's rudimentary code was to govern prize-fighting for almost a century.

THE RING

RULES

TO BE OBSERVED IN ALL BATTLES ON THE STAGE

I. That a square of a Yard be chalked in the middle of the Stage; and on every fresh set-to after a fall, or being parted from the rails, each Second is to bring his Man to the side of the square, and place him opposite to the other, and till they are fairly set-to at the Lines, it shall not be lawful for one to strike at the other.

II. That, in order to prevent any Disputes, the time a Man lies after a fall, if the Second does not bring his Man to the side of the square, within the space of half a minute, he shall be deemed a beaten Man.

III. That in every main Battle, no person whatever shall be upon the Stage, except the Principals and their Seconds; the same rule to be observed in bye-battles, except that in the latter, Mr. Broughton is allowed to be upon the Stage to keep decorum, and to assist Gentlemen in getting to their places, provided always he does not interfere in the Battle; and whoever pretends to infringe these Rules to be turned immediately out of the house. Every body is to quit the Stage as soon as the Champions are stripped, before the set-to.

IV. That no Champion be deemed beaten, unless he fails coming up to the line in the limited time, or that his own Second declares him beaten. No Second is to be allowed to ask his man's Adversary any questions, or advise him to give out.

V. That in bye-battles, the winning man to have two-thirds of the Money given, which shall be publicly divided upon the Stage, notwithstanding any private agreements to the contrary.

VI. That to prevent Disputes, in every main Battle the Principals shall, on coming on the Stage, choose from among the gentlemen present two Umpires, who shall absolutely decide all Disputes that may arise about the Battle; and if the two Umpires cannot agree, the said Umpires to choose a third, who is to determine it.

VII. That no person is to hit his Adversary when he is down, or seize him by the ham, the breeches, or any part below the waist: a man on his knees to be reckoned down.

As agreed by several Gentlemen at Broughton's Amphitheatre, Tottenham Court Road, August 16, 1743.

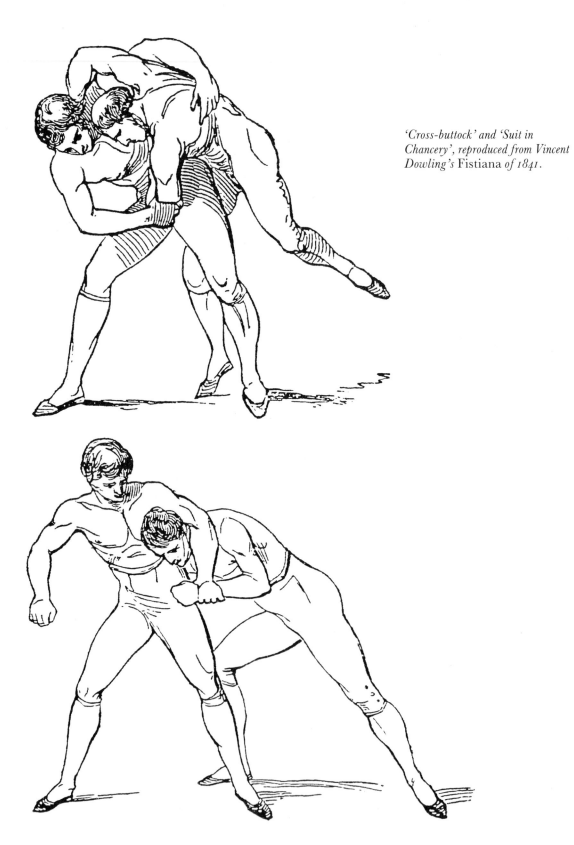

'Cross-buttock' and 'Suit in Chancery', reproduced from Vincent Dowling's Fistiana *of 1841.*

GLOSSARY

Bottom	Courage or 'guts'
Cly or Clie	Pocket
Cross	Sometimes rendered as 'X' by Egan. A fixed or thrown fight. 'Why is the late fight between Josh Hudson and the Caulker like the top of St Paul's? – Because it is a Grand Cross.' *Bell's Life*, 1822.
Cross-buttock	'A particular lock or fall in the Broughtonian Art, which, as Mr Fielding observes, conveyed more pleasant sensations to the spectators than the patient.' *Dictionary of the Vulgar Tongue*, 1811. The object of this throw was to end a round by pitching an opponent over the buttocks to the ground.
Daffy	Gin, the favourite beverage of the Fancy, also known as Blue Ruin, a Flash of Lightning and Stark Naked.
Daffy Club	A less affluent version of the Pugilistic Club which met at the Castle Tavern, Holborn.
Fib	A short or Half-arm punch.
Flat	An innocent gull or 'Johnny Raw'.
Mufflers or Muffles	Boxing gloves used in sparring matches. '. . . a black eye in a recent scuffle, For sometimes we must box without the muffle.' Byron, *Don Juan*, 1818–20.
PC	Pugilistic Club: a subscription club founded in 1814, for the promotion and regulation of fights. The clubs' corner stakes were painted with the letters, which were also engraved into the waistcoat buttons of PC members, employed to 'beat out' the ring before and sometimes during a fight.
Steven, Blunt or Brads	Money
Stump the Brads	Put up the money.
Suit in Chancery	To grasp an opponents head under one arm, whilst leaving the other free to 'fib'.
Turn-up	A casual or unscheduled fight.

CHAPTER 1

HARD MEN AND
PAST TIMES

It was the one time in his life, in the House or out of it, that he ever spoke with eagerness and almost with passion . . . He said that his conviction of the advantages of pugilism was so strong that he had been seriously considering whether it was not a duty that he owed to the public to go and attend every prizefight which took place, and thus to encourage the noble science to the extent of his power . . . He described the fight between Gully and the Chicken – how he rode down to Brickhill himself, and was loitering about the inn door, when a barouche and four drove up with Lord Byron and a party, and Jackson, the trainer – how they all dined together, and how pleasant it had been. Next day came the fight, and he described the men stripping, the intense excitement, the sparring, then the first round, and the attitudes of the men – it was really worthy of Homer.

JOHN EVELYN DENISON,
A CONVERSATION WITH JOHN, 3RD EARL SPENCER OF ALTHORP, c1840

John Gully and Hen Pearce, 'The Game Chicken', square up to each other, on the base of Lord Byron's dressing screen. Byron had painstakingly cut these figures from individual etchings published by Lopez in 1805, the year in which the great fight between the pair had been witnessed by the poet, together with Viscount Althorp and the future King William IV.
REPRODUCED BY COURTESY OF
JOHN MURRAY LTD.

When, in early Victorian England, an aristocratic parliamentarian chose to reminisce with another distinguished public servant about the carefree days of their youth, it was quite natural that the conversation should, sooner or later, turn to pugilism. Lord Althorp, an ancester of the present Princess of Wales, had been a very keen boxer at Harrow, as was his schoolfellow, George Byron. This taste for the Noble Art was to develop beyond schooldays when both their Lordships, in common with about one-third of the peerage, were to receive boxing lessons from ex-champion John Jackson at his fashionable Bond Street establishment. It was entirely in keeping with the spirit of the age in which they grew to manhood that two such pugilistically inclined young lords should be proud to have supped with their accomplished friend and teacher, on the eve of a truly epic fight, in the great years of pugilism. No less appropriate is the fact that Althorp, as heir to one of the world's finest classical libraries, should consider the occasion on which a pair of English bruisers battered each other for sixty-four bloody rounds in a prosaically damp Sussex meadow as subject matter worthy of the greatest among ancient authors.

In *The Illiad*, probably written at some time during the eighth century BC, Homer had supplied the earliest extant description of a prize-fight, a thrilling battle in which Epeios beat Euryalos with leather-bound fists, at the funeral games of the hero Patrokles. While other Greek authors, including Plato and Pindar were to honour boxers and the practice of boxing, the next most famous classical prize-fight description after that of Homer occurs in *The Aeneid* by the Roman poet Virgil. Writing in the first century BC, Virgil's verses describe the downfall of a boastful young Dares at the hands of wily 'old pro' Entellus.

The boxing matches of ancient Greek and Roman mythology usually ended with the 'breaking of bones' and much 'spitting of clotted blood', to the intense satisfaction of the spectators who, from a safe distance, evinced every bit as strong a predilection for gore as do their present-day counterparts. Even so, a far more sinister note had been sounded when, in the story of *The Golden Fleece*, the mythical Greek boxer Polydeuces, better known by his Roman name of Pollux, was forced to fight for his life against the homicidal King Amycus in a contest which foreshadowed the bloody gladiatorial circuses of Imperial Rome.

Boxing is among the earliest of sports to be described in literature, and it certainly holds a similarly pre-eminent position in the history of the visual arts. There are six-thousand-year-old representations of something resembling a fist-fight from both Egypt and Mesopotamia, but the drawing is vague and leaves a lot to the imagination. We have to move forward in time to the Minoan civilisation of about 1600 BC, before we come to the earliest indisputable depictions of boxing. A Minoan vase from Ayia Triadha in Crete, known as the 'Boxer Rython', shows pairs of opponents, some of whom are standing in lively poses whilst others have fallen or been knocked down. At about the same period from the volcanic island of Thera to the north of Crete comes the well-known, though much restored, mural painting of two youths, who actually appear to be making fist to head contact. From this period onwards, through archaic and classical Greece, down to the virtual collapse of the Roman empire, the representation of boxing matches on vases or wall paintings and in sculpture and mosaic became widespread throughout the lands of Western civilisation.

Great impetus was gained by the art and literature of boxing, no less than by the sport itself, with the advent at Olympia and elsewhere of public games in which valuable prizes were offered for competition. The actual history, as opposed to the mythology, of prize-fighting can be said to date from the introduction of boxing into the Olympic Games of 688 BC, where one Onamastus of Smyrna emerged as first champion. Odes were composed and statues raised to succeeding champions, including men such as Milo of Croton and Theogenes of Thebes, who were so revered that history and myth once more become confused in the recounting of their exploits.

Forty years after the introduction of boxing into the Olympic calendar, there appeared a curious event called the Pankration, named from the Greek adjective *pankrates*, meaning 'all-powerful'. This innovation, which combined elements of boxing, wrestling and judo, in some ways foreshadowed English pugilism, with its bare-handed grappling and cross-buttock throws. But, unlike either English or ancient boxing, the pankration continued on the ground after a fall, the contestants wrestling, punching and kicking until one or the other gave in. Yet, despite the rather lax rules governing this event, boxing was still regarded as the really tough sport, and remained the more popular spectacle.

The purest ideal of ancient Olympic boxing was to hit an opponent whilst avoiding the returned blow, and many

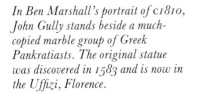

In Ben Marshall's portrait of c1810, John Gully stands beside a much-copied marble group of Greek Pankratiasts. The original statue was discovered in 1583 and is now in the Uffizi, Florence.

contests were distinguished by great skill. In the classical world, as later in Regency England, the representation in painting or sculpture of a handsome, unmarked face was a tribute to a clever boxer, one with the ability to ride or slip punches and to outdance his opponent. Slugging, however, remained the norm in bouts where contestants wore the ancient equivalent of boxing gloves – the cestus, a kind of leather thong which encased and protected the fist and forearm, at the expense of the head and face of the recipient of a blow. Accordingly, most bouts were inclined to be the somewhat bloody and brutal affairs, familiar from mythology. A degree of brutality is evident in the famous bronze figure of a boxer in the National Museum in Rome, who bears the scarred eyebrows, broken nose, cauliflower ears and disfigured mouth of the archetypal pug. This figure might well be

This life-sized bronze figure of a classical pugilist, from the National Museum in Rome, exhibits not only the physique necessary to his calling, but ox-hide bound fists and the consequent facial damage.

taken to represent the fictitious Stratophon, butt of a mocking epigram written by the Roman poet Lucillius in the time of the emperor Nero:

> When Odysseus came home after twenty years, his dog recognised him at once. But you, after a mere four hours' boxing are unrecognisable not only to dogs but to the city. Look in the mirror and you will say under oath, 'I am not Stratophon.'

What would Lucillius have said about the brutes portrayed at the third-century baths of Caracalla in Rome? Here the mosaic exudes barbarity as if to warn the onlooker that these ugly, shaven-headed gladiators, with their metal-spiked and studded cestii, exist simply to smash out the brains and entrails of other men for the gratification of a depraved public. Boxing had sunk to an all-time low, but continued unabated both as a gladiatorial show and as an Olympic event until the Christian Emperor Theodosius the Great abolished the Games in AD 393, from which time prize-fighting was to remain more or less unheard of for another thirteen centuries.

Occasional references to the English predilection for fist-fighting may be found in the literature of the Middle Ages, and the Florentine sculptor Torrigiano was later to boast of his boxing skill acquired in the England of Henry VIII, but boxing for a *prize* seems to have lain dormant from the time of the late Roman Empire until in the mid-seventeenth century it was rediscovered by certain English gentlemen with a taste for head-punching and the antique.

In 1637 there was published in London a curious collection of poems entitled: *Annalia Dubrensia: Upon the yeerely celebration of Mr Robert Dovers Olimpick Games upon Cotswold-Hills*. In this quaint little volume, which praises the revived games while comparing them to the Greek and Roman orginals, we are informed that:

> The warrelike Champion with his powerful fists,
> Contended for the Prize, as in our lists,

Our poet then hands the torch, as it were, to a colleague, who, in citing Virgil's pugilistic hero, leaves us in no doubt as to the inclusion of prize-boxing in Mr Dovers' 'Olimpick' programme, although mention of the 'Caestus' may probably be taken as poetic licence:

> *Entellus* he at *Caestus* had the best,
> In mighty strength surpassing all the rest.
> Such were the old World's sports; now transferr'd over
> Into our *Cotswold*, by thee, worthy DOVER.

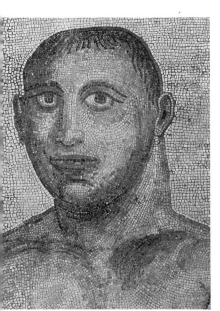

A brutally realistic mosaic portrait of a Roman boxer, from the early-third-century baths of Caracalla, in Rome.

Even if the standard of boxing was no better than the poetry, here is proof of fist-fighting for a prize in the reign of Charles I. Almost half a century would pass until, after the Civil War and the Restoration of the Monarchy, the first newspaper report of a boxing match appeared in the *Protestant Mercury* of January 1681.

Surprisingly, little more was then heard of boxing for another forty years, when its continuing existence and popularity was suddenly demonstrated by the erection of a 'ring' in Hyde Park 'by order of His Majesty'. This amenity, provided for the use of any member of the general public who required pugilistic satisfaction, seems to have been especially aimed at the ranks of bellicose chairmen and linkmen with whom the capital swarmed at this period. George Borrow was later to boast of his father fighting here with no less an opponent than Big Ben Brain, the future champion! Such a scene had been witnessed by the astonished French visitor de Saussure who, writing in 1727, explains that when two working men have a disagreement which they cannot settle amicably, they often:

> Retire into some quiet place and strip from their waists upwards. Everyone who sees them preparing for a fight surrounds them, not in order to separate them, but on the contrary to enjoy the fight, for it is a great sport to the lookers-on, and they judge the blows and also help to enforce certain rules in use for this mode of warfare. The spectators sometimes get so interested that they lay bets on the combatants and form a big circle around them. The two champions shake hands before commencing, and then attack each other courageously with their fists, and sometimes also with their heads, which they use like rams. Should one of the men fall, his opponent may, according to the rules, give him a blow with his fist, but those who have laid their bets on the fallen man generally encourage him to continue till one of the combatants is quite knocked up and says he has had enough.

The consistently amazed Frenchman had also reported the readiness with which many English gentlemen were willing to lay aside sword and wig to fight in the street with the notoriously aggressive and disrespectful lower orders. In the resulting species of rough democracy which prevailed in the jostling thoroughfares and unlit alleyways of Georgian London, proficiency in the martial arts became a social necessity, and schools which taught gentlemen the rudiments of self-defence began to flourish all over the capital. The most popular of these establishments was that which had been opened near the Tottenham Court Road by James Figg in 1719. It was within this highly successful school that Captain Godfrey, British boxing's first scribe, tells us, 'I purchased my

James Figg clutches a pair of quarter-staffs while looking with distaste at M. Dubois, the fencing master, and the other 'artists and professors' who surround the young rake, in Hogarth's A Rake's Progress *of 1735.*

knowledge with many a broken head and bruises in every part of me.'

Figg, who was himself best known for his prowess with sword and quarterstaff, employed a regular troupe of boxers to demonstrate their skill, and to take on all-comers. One of Figg's paid entourage was a boxer named George Taylor who, following the sudden death of his employer in 1734, took over the management and turned his attention fully to boxing. A few years later Taylor was beaten in his own booth by Jack Broughton, another of Figg's protégés, who was destined to become the founder of the English prize-ring, and is still known as 'The Father of Boxing'.

By the beginning of 1743, Broughton had opened his own 'amphitheatre' which, under the patronage of William, Duke of Cumberland, was completely to overshadow all similar enterprises, including that of the neighbouring Taylor. It was from these premises that later in the same year Broughton published the first rules of boxing, which were to govern the sport for almost a century. Within a few years Broughton's popularity enabled him to contemplate a move to larger and smarter premises, where he was to introduce 'muffles', as boxing gloves were then known. An advertisement which appeared in the *Daily Advertiser* on 1 February 1747 explains the reasons for this concession to civilisation:

> Mr Broughton proposes, with proper assistance, to open an academy at his house in the Hay-Market, for the instruction of those who are willing to be initiated in the mystery of boxing: where the whole theory and practice of that truly British art, with all the various stops, blows, cross buttocks, &c. incident to combatants, will be fully taught and explain'd; and that persons of quality and distinction may not be deterred from entering into a *Course of these Lectures*, they will be given with the utmost tenderness and regard to the delicacy of the frame and constitution of the pupil, for which reason muffles are provided, that will effectually secure them from the inconveniency of black eyes, broken jaws, and bloody noses.

Notwithstanding this comforting assurance, bare-knuckles remained *de rigeur* for prize-fights between professionals, and it was due to this mode of combat that the sadly out-of-condition Broughton suffered a surprise defeat at the hands of Jack Slack, whose sharp knuckles temporarily blinded the old champion, to end his career in 1750.

The years of Broughton's ascendancy had coincided with a period in which the sword had ceased to be a fashionable dress accessory among the English gentry. Indeed, to be seen wearing one now constituted an affront to the proletariat; some foreign visitors had even been forced to stand by

Jack Broughton, mezzotint of c1740 engraved by Faber, from an oil painting by John Ellys, originally published as a pair with a similar portrait of James Figg. Ellys had been a fellow-student, with Hogarth, of Sir James Thornhill. All three artists were to produce portraits of leading boxers.

helplessly while their lethal symbol of superiority was snapped across the knee of some big-boned, equality conscious butcher. Despite the popularity gained by boxing during this period, the embryonic prize-ring suffered a serious setback following Broughton's defeat and the disillusioned Duke of Cumberland's consequent withdrawal of patronage. From this time onwards the sport was to continue more or less illegally for the remainder of its days.

Following a period of bribery and chicanery, prestige returned to the ring during the 1780s when the championships of Tom Johnson and Daniel Mendoza coincided with a restoration of royal patronage by the Prince of Wales and his entourage. Local magistrates were understandably inclined to turn a blind eye to any illegal event at which HRH and half the nobility were present, while at the same time the honesty and exemplary behaviour, outside the ring, of champions like John Jackson and Hen Pearce added lustre to a once again thriving spectator sport.

Prize-fighting reached the height of its popularity during this time. New, more rapid and skilful techniques were introduced by the Belcher brothers at the beginning of the nineteenth century, and the craze for pugilism continued unabated for the next twenty-five years, a period covered largely by the careers of Tom Cribb and his protégé, Tom Spring. A steady decline set in with the retirement of Spring in 1824; bribery again became commonplace and many fights ended in general brawling and the withholding of bets and stake-money.

Deaths in the ring became increasingly frequent during the 1830s, and much adverse publicity was attracted by the championship bout of 1833, in which Simon Byrne was fatally injured by Deaf Burke. Broughton's Rules were overhauled in 1838, but the relatively humane 'New Rules', of course, did nothing to stop the dishonesty with which pugilism had by now become infested. The prize-ring's lowest ebb was perhaps marked by the two Ben Caunt versus Bendigo contests of 1838 and 1845, both of which ended with disqualification and a full-scale riot.

An unexpected pugilistic revival occurred at the time of the great international match between Sayers and Heenan in 1860, but it was really a final flaring up of an outmoded way of life, and English prize-fighting fizzled out soon after. The best fighters then emigrated across the Atlantic, to the more lax social climate which prevailed throughout the United States in the aftermath of civil war.

The practice of bare-knuckle pugilism, along with its exponents and the spectators, should be seen and judged against a squalid and brutal social background. In our comparatively soft times it is easy to forget that the days of fighting for supper are still within living memory, and that the possibility of a beating in the ring once paled beside the very real experience of hunger and grinding poverty. The living conditions endured by the poor, and made familiar to us through the writings of Charles Dickens, were a nineteenth-century fact of life, which the great author had to expurgate and play down to facilitate publication.

The period during which English pugilism had flourished was an age of violent excesses and contrasts, of vulgar refinement and facile manners. On one hand a young man of fortune could win, or more likely lose, thousands of pounds in an evening at one of London's many fashionable gaming 'hells', while at the same time farm workers were transported to penal colonies on the other side of the world for the 'crime' of forming a union to protest at the reduction of their weekly wage from nine shillings to six.

In 1833 the recommended working day for a labourer under the age of thirteen was reduced by Parliament to ten hours. Small boys were still forced to climb up and sweep the insides of soot-filled chimneys, at the risk not only of broken bones, but of fatal pulmonary infections and various forms of cancer.

Small girls fared no better than the boys, and the fate of many can easily be imagined. Crime was an attractive and more lucrative alternative to the prevailing conditions of employment, and criminal activity was correspondingly high.

In the early part of the nineteenth century there were still over 160 offences in the criminal code for which the death penalty could be imposed, and what we would regard as minor crimes were regularly punished by major sentences. The final public execution in England did not take place until as late as 1868, right at the end of the age of pugilism and halfway through the enlightened and supposedly Christian reign of Queen Victoria the Good.

Back in the England of the later eighteenth century a number of quite disparate trends and tendencies had coincided, as a result of which the phenomenon of pugilism caught the popular imagination and the prize-ring became enshrined as the symbol of an age.

The neo-classical cognoscenti had been busily rediscovering the art and literature of classical Greece and Rome. In these civilisations the heroic and skilful, though still robust, boxing match had been eulogised by their finest writers, while the noble boxer had been portrayed in bronze or marble and worshipped as a god. The very terms used to describe the practice of boxing are taken from these resurrected civilisations. The word pugilism is derived from the Latin *pugil* – a boxer, and *pugnare* – to fight. The etymology of the word 'box' is rather obscure, but it is probably derived from the Greek *pyx* – with the fist.

We have seen how the shedding of swords by gentlemen had contributed to a kind of street democracy, and perhaps boxing may be viewed as a subconscious egalitarian alternative to the deadly aristocratic practice of duelling, still fashionable on the Continent.

The period had witnessed a huge movement of population from rural areas into the new industrial manufacturing centres. Dwellers in overcrowded cities, who from earliest childhood have had to fight for the basic commodities of life, tend of necessity to be swifter of reaction and more aggressive than their country cousins and forebears, and it was from the slums and tenements of the new conurbations that the majority of fighters were to come.

At the same time new concepts of egalitarianism combined with a fear of the mob, engendered by the bloody social upheavals then occurring in revolutionary France, encouraged the English upper classes to extol the virtues of the common man and to patronise his physical prowess. A quality possessed by all the best boxers was 'bottom', a combination of what we should call 'guts' with coolness of judgement. This indispensible attribute was an echo of the phlegmatism encouraged by the emergent public schools, and it must have been comforting for both rich and poor to see that those at the other end of the social scale subscribed to the same ethos. If the boxing ring could be seen as a framework within which the potentially destructive power of the underprivileged was to be contained through a collaborative activity, then there was a chance of avoiding the extremes to which theoretically less happy nations had been driven.

In times of war the army had always provided an outlet for plebean violence, by simply posting abroad what the reactionary Duke of Wellington had been pleased to call 'the scum of the earth'. But the release, if only temporary, of the rank and file of a huge army required a safety valve to disperse some of the remaining pent-up aggression. This was partly provided, as was the case during and after two world wars in our own century, by an upsurge in the staging of boxing tournaments.

During the first two decades of the nineteenth century Great Britain was to emerge from many years of almost constant war with France as a world power of unprecedented magnitude and almost unparalleled self-esteem. The Englishman's belief in his superior physical prowess was but one manifestation of this hard-won national pre-eminence. William Hazlitt, writing ten years after Waterloo, informs us:

A wood engraving from De Arte Gymnastica, *printed in Italy in 1573, presents the Renaissance view of ancient boxing.*

There are two things that an Englishman understands, hard words and hard blows. Nothing short of this (generally speaking) excites his attention or interests him in the least. His neighbours have the benefit of the one in war time, and his own countrymen of the other in the time of peace. The French express themselves astonished at the feats which our Jack Tars have so often performed. A fellow in that class of life in England will strike his hand through a deal board – first, to show his strength, which he is proud of; secondly, to give him a sensation, which he is want of; lastly, to prove his powers of endurance, which he also makes a boast of.

The English do not hold up their heads, but they will turn their backs on no man: they delight in doing and in bearing more than others: what every one else shrinks from through aversion to labour or pain, they are attracted to, and go through with, and so far (and so far only) they are a great people. At least it cannot be denied they are a *pugnacious* set. Their heads are so full of this that if a Frenchman speaks of Scribe, the celebrated farce writer, a young Englishman present will suppose he means Cribb the boxer; and ten thousand people assembled at a prize-fight will witness an exhibition of pugilism with the same breathless attention and delight as the audience at the *Théâtre Français* listen to the dialogue of Racine or Molière. Assuredly, we do not pay the same attention to Shakespeare; but at a boxing match every Englishman feels his power to give and take blows increased by sympathy, as at a French theatre every spectator fancies that the actors on the stage talk, laugh, and make love as he would.

These views were readily endorsed over the following half century, by sporting journalists such as Vincent Dowling:

> The annals of our country from the invasion of the Romans downwards sufficiently demonstrate that the native Briton trusted more to the strength of his arm, the muscular vigour of his frame, and the fearless attributes of his mind in the hour of danger, than to any artificial expedients; and that, whether in attack or defence, the combination of those qualities rendered him at all times formidable in the eyes of his assailants, however skilled in the science or practice of warfare. If illustrations were required to establish this proposition, they are to be found in every page of our history, from the days of Alfred to the battle of Waterloo; and if it be asked how it is that Englishmen stand thus pre-eminent in the eyes of the world, it may be answered that it is to be ascribed to the encouragement given to those manly games (boxing more especially) which are characteristic of their country, and which, while they invigorate the system, sustain and induce that moral courage which experience has shown us to be the result as much of education as of constitution.

The prize-ring was frequently used as a metaphor for political debate. This cartoon of 1798 shows Charles James Fox 'tapping the Claret' of William Pitt, while the Commons look on and comment approvingly.
REPRODUCED BY COURTESY OF G. ROSE.

What a contrast between honest, hard-hitting John Bull and his effete national adversary from across the English Channel! It was not only the French that attracted unfavourable comparison: the back-stabbing Spaniard, stilletto-carrying Italian, bludgeon-wielding Dutchman and Bowie-knife-touting American all come in for their share of censure and ridicule. The literature of the period is riddled with statements of outrageous national prejudice, sentiments which seem to have been wholeheartedly endorsed by the majority of Englishmen, to the enduring astonishment of the rest of the world. The early-nineteenth-century American author, Washington Irving, was to observe that:

> Men are apt to acquire peculiarities that are continually ascribed to them . . . the common orders of the English seem wonderfully captivated with the *beau ideal* which they have formed of John Bull, and endeavour to act up to the caricature that is perpetually held up before their eyes.

It was not just the 'common orders' who were thus captivated. In 1809, at the height of the Peninsular War, the Rt Hon. William Windham, Secretary for War and the Colonies, and patron of pugilism, having returned to his duties after attending a prize-fight in east Kent, had written:

A smart contest this, between Maddox and Richmond! Why are we to boast so much of the native valour of our troops, as shown at Talavera, at Vimiero, and at Marida, yet to discourage all the practices and habits which tend to keep alive the same sentiments and feelings? The sentiments that filled the minds of three thousand spectators who witnessed those two pugilists were the same in kind as those which inspired the higher combatants on the occasions before enumerated. It is the circumstances only in which they are displayed that make the difference.

During this time of acute, if sometimes comic, xenophobia occurred one of the most far-reaching social unpheavals in our history, a complex series of interconnected events which for convenience are labelled 'The Industrial Revolution'. The fears and aspirations of the machine age were expressed by Mary Shelly when she wrote *Frankenstein* in 1817. Many people at the time believed that mankind was, like Dr Frankenstein, in grave danger of allowing the machine, a monster of his own creation, to get out of control and totally dictate the lives and actions of men. The 'dark satanic mills' of the new Jerusalem were in danger of dehumanising into

robots the workers, or 'hands', as they had become known, hands whose every move was geared to the increasing demands of screaming, smoke-belching machinery, punctuated by factory hooters.

Against this background of conflict and social strife, and perhaps as a reaction to it, physical sports and 'manly games' were enjoying a huge revival. Boxing in particular was seen by many from all walks of life as a form both of national and social self-expression.

Writing in 1812, Pierce Egan recommends his newly published magnum opus, *Boxiana*:

> ... to those people who feel that Englishmen are not automatons; and however necessary discipline may be for the precision and movement of great bodies, that it would be of non-effect, were it not animated by a native spirit, producing that love of country, which has been found principally to originate from what the fastidious term – vulgar sports!

Whether or not we agree with Egan's reasoning, the fact remains that certain vulgar sports and sportsmen were becoming national institutions.

The leading fighters at the time of the Industrial Revolution and Napoleonic Wars were the first genuine working-class heroes to be revered as such. Previously, heroes who could boast no lordly genealogy very swiftly had one invented for them by the writers of the day. Even Robin Hood had been raised to the peerage as 'Robin of Locksley, dispossessed Saxon Earl of Huntingdon', whereas 'that robbin' peasant in a hood' seems far more plausible. Dick Turpin and the other highwaymen of the seventeenth and eighteenth centuries, although in fact of humble birth, were presented to a gullible public as gentlemen who through no fault of their own had fallen on hard times.

Now, in contrast, national hero Tom Cribb, on nodding terms with poets and princes, was known and admitted to be an illiterate Gloucestershire coal-whipper turned publican. Always at his most dangerous when 'milling on the retreat' or apparently beaten, Cribb personified British pluck and tenacity. His name, which was a byword for bravery and fair play, exuded the same nationalist charisma as those of his well-bred contemporaries, Nelson and Wellington. Out of an anonymous and fast-vanishing agricultural world was slowly and painfully emerging the age of the common man, while at the same time the stifling conformity of the Neo-Classical eighteenth century was giving way to a Romantic idolisation of individual sensibility. Both of these parallel trends found their ideal expression in the lionising of the prize-fighter as popular hero.

Few modern boxers have aspired to the prominent position in our society that the bruisers of the Regency maintained in theirs. A more apt modern comparison would perhaps be with the working-class actors and pop singers of the 'swinging sixties', whose style of dress and even speech was aped by the unfashionable middle and upper classes. In the early nineteenth century, gentlemen and noblemen boxed, swore and wore their neckties 'à la Belcher' in honour of a celebrated Bristol butcher's boy, turned bruiser, who, in any other age, would have been beneath their contempt.

The renown enjoyed by the leading prize-fighters in this age of 'Boximania' was, however, ambivalent. Fêted by members of the aristocracy and deified within large sections of the working class as the personification of Englishness, they were held in awe, but never considered quite respectable, by the majority of the population. The appearance of bruiser and future MP, John Gully, among the fashionable audience at the Drury Lane Theatre had attracted adverse comment in 1807, and in *The Romany Rye* fight-fan George Borrow even had a gypsy girl speak disparagingly about the social desirability of top-flight boxer Tom Oliver.

The basic differences between prize-fighting under Broughton's Rules of 1743, or the 1838 Rules of the Pugilistic Association, and boxing as practised within the code first published by the 8th Marquess of Queensbury in 1867, are as follows: in the former, contestants fought with bare knuckles until one or both were knocked down, thrown, or fell from exhaustion, which signified the end of the round. Certain wrestling throws were permitted and a round was far more likely to end with a 'cross-buttock' than with a clean knock-down. After thirty seconds, 'Time' was called and the combatants had a further eight seconds to 'come up to scratch', which was a line marked in the centre of the ring. Either man failing to do so was deemed to have lost the contest, or to have been 'knocked out' of time. These fights were always to the finish, they could not be won or lost on points.

In contrast Queensbury decreed the wearing of padded gloves of a certain size, a specific number of timed rounds, with a timed rest period between them. In the case of a knockdown the fallen man has ten seconds to rise to his feet or be counted out, while hugging and wrestling of any description is definitely forbidden.

The idea of padded gloves was to protect the contestants from the more spectacular facial injuries, which had been accepted as part and parcel of the game by spectators of the bare-knuckle era, who even placed bets not only on the result of the fight but on 'first blood' and 'first knockdown'. In reality gloves also afford protection to the hands of the striker, which, when combined with the tapes and bandages used in modern boxing, become weapons allowing a fighter to hit with a power and repetition unknown in the old prize-ring. Fighting with bare knuckles involved much body-punching, the purpose of which was to sap the stamina of an opponent. Body-punching also placed the hands at less risk than careless or repeated blows to the head. Broken hands were, nevertheless, quite a common feature of the prize-ring.

Damage to the brain is far more likely to be produced by a gloved than an ungloved fist, so it is possible that the modern boxer and fight fan are being decoyed into a false sense of security by the apparent lack of damage evident at the end of contest terminating with a points decision. There have been various propositions tabled in recent years on 'medical grounds' for a return to the good old days of bare knuckles, but most modern audiences, sheltered since childhood from many of the more brutal facts of life, would be far too squeamish to endure the sort of two-hour bloodbath so heartily relished by their recent forebears.

Timed rounds and a system of point-scoring were introduced to speed up proceedings, as fights under the old rules had often degenerated into hugging and mauling matches of several hours' duration. These contests were finally decided by the sheer exhaustion of one or both of the participants, and, one would suspect, by that of the spectators only a little less.

Whereas now a championship contest is usually scheduled for twelve or fifteen three-minute rounds, totalling thirty-six or forty-five minutes actual fighting time, under the old system the number of rounds fought is no indication whatever of the actual duration of a contest.

In 1817 Jack Randall beat Aby Belasco in fifty-five minutes, during which time only seven rounds were fought. Two years later Randall was to beat Jack Martin in nineteen rounds occupying forty-nine minutes. It should be pointed out that Randall, 'The Nonpareil', was considered a quick finisher, only one opponent ever lasting more than an hour, on which occasion in 1818 it had taken him two hours, nineteen minutes and thirty-four rounds to dispose of the tough and skilful Ned Turner. In contrast, slow but sure Tom Sayers fought for two hours or more on no less than six occasions, one of them a gruelling contest against Harry Paulson, lasting for 109 rounds and occupying three hours and eight minutes. Sayers had finished off the opponent previous to Paulson in four rounds lasting only five minutes, but prize-fights could generally be expected to continue for between one and two hours.

Another contrast between the bare-knuckle and gloved eras is the number of contests engaged in by each fighter. Today a professional boxer might be expected to have between forty and sixty fights during a successful career. Henry Cooper had fifty-five spread over seventeen years. Gloved fighters of the previous generation usually had many more; for instance, Tommy Farr took part in 125 fights over twenty-seven years and Len Harvey 134 in twenty-two years. The comparable bare-knuckle bruisers averaged about one fight a year in a career spanning perhaps a dozen years. Tom Cribb had a total of only eleven contests over a seven-year period, and Tom Sayers fought fourteen times in eleven years. Clearly a fight to the finish takes more out of the human physique than a points win over a few three-minute rounds.

There were, of course, exceptions to this norm. For instance 'Paddington' Tom Jones took part in about twenty fights spread over nineteen years, whilst his namesake Harry Jones fought an unprecedented thirty-four times in thirteen years. At the other end of the scale the two great Johns, Jackson and Gully, fought their way to fame and fortune with only three fights apiece, of which they each lost one, but then they were both exceptional men in every way.

It must be remembered that the foregoing figures refer to fights which took place in the regular prize-ring, into which nobody had the temerity or the opportunity to step without first discovering an aptitude for the game in numerous provincial skirmishes. A present-day parallel is the youth who decides to turn professional, having first proved himself in the amateur ranks.

The object of prize-fighting was to hit your opponent, while at the same time avoiding his return blow. This ritual was enacted ideally in the presence of a large and vociferous crowd, who placed bets on the outcome and from whom gate money could be extracted, but there any resemblance to modern boxing ends. Prize-fighting was a different game, fought to different rules and existing within a different world: a world in which germ warfare and the neutron bomb would have been as unthinkable as the close-quarter carnage of Trafalgar and Waterloo is unacceptable to us.

The tailpiece to the bound volume of Punch *for January to June 1860 leaves little doubt that* The London Charivari *considered the fight between Sayers and Heenan to have been the single most newsworthy event of that half-year.*
REPRODUCED BY COURTESY OF *PUNCH*.

CHAPTER 2

PUGS AND PAINTERS

> *Michelangelo's nose was flat from a blow which he received in his youth from Torrigiano, a brother artist and countryman, who gave me the following account of the occurrence: 'I was,' said Torrigiano, 'extremely irritated, and, doubling my fist, gave him such a violent blow on the nose that I felt the cartilages yield as if they had been made of paste, and the mark I then gave him he will carry to the grave'. . . Torrigiano . . . was continually talking about his great feats among 'those bears of Englishmen' whose country he had lately quitted.*
>
> BENVENUTO CELLINI, *AUTOBIOGRAPHY*, 1558–66.

Richard Humphries 'The Celebrated Boxer who never was Conquered'. A portrait in oils, commissioned by the boxers' leading patron from John Hoppner. The fashionable engraver John Young then produced this striking mezzotint, which was published in 1788, within four days of Humphries' victory over up-and-coming Dan Mendoza.

Thus was the practice of boxing justified by Henry Downes Miles, the author of *Pugilistica*. He goes on to ask how great would have been mankind's loss had Torrigiano employed the cowardly stiletto usually favoured by his countrymen rather than the honest clenched fist, which he had learnt to use whilst working and brawling in Westminster. The same writer omits the fact that Torrigiano was boasting about a youthful escapade which had occurred long before his first visit to pugnacious England. However, most readers of *Pugililstica* would not have questioned the author's point.

By the time that recourse to the Italian Renaissance was considered necessary to justify the 'Old English' practice of nose-breaking, prize-fighting and its exponents had been firing the imagination of artists for 150 years. The reasons are in some instances obvious, in others less so.

A well-attended prize fight was a visually exciting event, which combined all the colour and glamour of any other great public occasion, with an extra ingredient: the probability of sudden and violent climax. In addition, the foremost fighters of the time were regarded by the general public with a degree of awe, then more usually reserved for war heroes, or today lavished on popular musicians.

Worshipped by the mob and petted by aristocrats, pugilists were portrayed as demi-gods by many fashionable and famous artists. At the same time, it seems likely that some wealthy backers of the prize-ring considered their pet boxers to be on a par with the prize cattle which roamed their country estates. These patrons were willing to pay high prices in order to adorn the walls of their mansions with good quality paintings of prize bulls and prize bruisers, picturesquely posed in romantically landscaped parkland.

A large number of the men who considered fighting a means of livelihood were of necessity physically very well developed. They therefore made excellent models for the kind of subject matter very much in demand during an age which was enthusiastically rediscovering the art of classical Greece. The sport of boxing was itself seen by some learned members of Georgian society as a revival of the Olympic ideal, a semi-nude contest of strength, skill and agility. 'Standing at the Academy', as modelling was known, brought many prize-fighters into close contact with artists, and at a time when sparring was considered a highly fashionable pursuit, some athletic academicians were more than happy to don the gloves with 'Hercules' or 'Odysseus'.

Sir Thomas Lawrence, President of the Royal Academy and the most fashionable painter of Regency society, used John Jackson's muscular figure as a model on several occasions. Sir Thomas had been considered a skilful boxer and was said to have sparred with Jackson in his youth. Jackson was to become Champion of England by employing the dubious tactic of holding the long hair of Daniel Mendoza with one hand, whilst beating him unconscious with the other. We may assume that 'Gentleman Jackson' had resisted the temptation to grab the luxurient chestnut locks which hung in Mendo-zaesque curls about the youthful painter's neck!

In stark contrast to the rich and famous Lawrence, his contemporary, George Moreland, the well-known painter of rural scenes, was never to fulfil his early promise as an artist. George was a crony of Joe Ward, a popular ex-pug turned teacher of the noble art. At his Soho pub, the Green Dragon, 'Old Joe', as he was known, kept a unique pugilistic art gallery in which were to be found:

> Portraits of nearly all the Pugilists (many of them in whole-lengths and attitudes) . . . from the days of Figg and Broughton down to the present period [1812]: with a variety of paintings of several of the most celebrated pugilistic encounters that have transpired, and likenesses of distinguished amateurs; . . . in short a very large room is filled from top to bottom, and as a proof of Ward's liberality in preserving the heroes of the fist, many of whom must have sunk into oblivion, he has had several painted at his own expense.

The recalcitrant features of Joe Ward, publican, retired pugilist, crony of George Moreland and unlikely patron of the arts.

As it was not, at this time, considered to be beneath the dignity of well-known artists to paint pub signs and the like, it is fascinating to conjecture whether Moreland was ever prevailed upon to demonstrate his considerable drawing skill in payment of his 'slate' by depicting any of these heroes of the fist. If so, what happened to the results, when, following Ward's death, his 'Cabinet of the Fancy' was sold by raffle?

Young George Moreland was reputed to have been a keen boxer; he most certainly was an even keener drinker, a factor which was to contribute to his tragically early death at the age of thirty-nine. The fate of Moreland brings to mind a statement made by the notorious 'Chief Baron', Renton Nicholson. Writing later in the nineteenth century from bitter experience he warns:

> As a rule, the acquaintance with fighting men should be avoided. It is almost as destructive . . . as the intimacy with profligate women.

One artist who seems to have revelled in the company of members of both these categories, without sustaining any lasting damage, was William Hogarth.

James Figg's business card, a copper engraving of c1720, by the fighter's friend, William Hogarth. Although by no means one of the artist's most accomplished productions, ephemeral work of this nature illustrates the kind of mundane commission once undertaken by even the most established artists.

Will.   Hogarth

James Figg
Master of y Noble-Science of Defence
on y right hand in Oxford Road
near Adam & Eve court. teaches Gentle-
men y use of y small. backsword. &
Quarterstaff. at home & abroad

Hogarth, generally regarded as the founder of the English school of painting, was an associate of James Figg, who held a similar place in the English school of self-defence. In about 1720 Hogarth designed and engraved a trade card, advertising Figg's Amphitheatre, which stood near what is now the junction of Oxford Street and Tottenham Court Road. In this uncharacteristically crude engraving the proprietor is shown, shaven-headed, standing on a railed and boarded stage, stripped to his shirt and holding a sword. Behind him stands his alter ego, in a pose remarkably like that which Hogarth was later to use in 'A Rake's Progress', where Figg again appears wearing a fashionable long wig and clutching a pair of quarterstaffs, whilst scowling at the duellist and other spongers who were deemed necessary appendages to every young man of taste during the reigns of the first two Georges.

Figg appears yet again in the foreground of Hogarth's 'Southwark Fair', at which unruly event the prize-fighter annually exhibited his knowledge of foil, back-sword, cudgel and fist. Of greater interest from the point of the pugilistic history is an easily overlooked scene in the background of Hogarth's 'The March to Finchley'. Painted in 1746, this is one of the very earliest representations of a prize-fight. A pair of shaven-headed bruisers are shown squaring up to each other, under the sign of The Adam and Eve, which had been Figg's address until his death in 1734 when ownership passed to George Taylor. 'The March to Finchley' seems to show two members of the team still practising at the old address, after Taylor had been forced to join Jack Broughton's more popular adjacent establishment. When Taylor died, after a fight, in 1758, Hogarth designed him the splendid tombstone described in Chapter Seven.

King George II was not amused by Hogarth's satire The march to Finchley, *which shows a drunken, whoreing army staggering north in 1745, to fight 'Bonny Prince Charlie'. The engraving contains one of the earliest English representations of a prize-fight.*

'The Set-to', a mezzotint by John Young after an oil painting attributed to John Hamilton Mortimer ARA, c1775. The majority of Mortimer's work exhibits the turbulence and torment usually associated with the Romanticism of the later eighteenth century. In contrast, the calm classical manner in which the artist chose to present such inherently violent subject-matter as a boxing match, suggests that this painting was copied from an earlier model.

Hogarth's penchant for the company of prize-fighters is again attested by several depictions of Jack Broughton, both in action and repose. One of the most interesting of these portraits was a representation of Broughton versus Slack, now unfortunately lost, which was probably produced as a ticket of admission to their famous fight of 1750. Broughton's famous shaven head and alert face were also depicted by many lesser artists than Hogarth. Perhaps the best known portrait is from an oil painting entitled 'The Set-To' by John Hamilton Mortimer. Painted thirty-five years after a contest which took place in 1741, 'The Set-To' shows Broughton, left hand and foot forward, about to engage with George Stevenson. This fatal fight probably prompted Broughton to draw up the first rudimentary rules of boxing in 1743. Why the artist should have chosen to paint an event which had taken place in the year of his own birth, or whether there is an earlier version which he used as a model, is not known. Maybe the young Mortimer had sparred with the ageing pugilist; we do know that the artist was a keen all-round sportsman, although he led a life of dissipation which foreshadowed that of George Moreland. Like Moreland, Mortimer died in his thirties.

Broughton, who is known to have posed for a statue of Hercules by the sculptor, Roubiliac, was also the subject of a lively drawing by George (later 4th Viscount and 1st Marquess) Townshend. Landowner, soldier, politician and earliest acknowledged English caricaturist, Townshend, when not ridiculing Broughton's patron, the Duke of Cumberland, found time to sketch the boxers, Jack Slack and Tom Smallwood, as well as Broughton himself.

The ageing Hogarth was to give vent to his hearty dislike of both Townshend and caricature, exclaiming that the latter had nothing to do with either art or skill, amusement being produced merely by the surprise that an arbitrary collection of lines and marks bore resemblance to anything whatever. Although, of course, never on the same plane as Hogarth's

The ageing Jack Broughton in action, a lively pen and ink sketch of about 1750, by George Townshend.
REPRODUCED BY COURTESY OF THE
NATIONAL PORTRAIT GALLERY, LONDON.

best work, it must be said that the action drawing of these boxers, Broughton in particular, easily stands comparison with Hogarth's engraving of Figg's card.

George Townshend had served as a soldier in Germany, where he commanded a brigade under the Marquis of Granby. An amusing story about the Marquis was often narrated by humourist, bon viveur and founding member of The Royal Academy, the painter Francis Hayman. Commissioned to paint a 'Hall of British Worthies' for display at Vauxhall Gardens, Hayman, who had earlier portrayed Jack Broughton, requested the honour of a sitting from the Marquis:

> In consequence, the hero of Minden dropped in at the artist's studio in St Martin's Lane. 'But, Frank,' said the peer, 'before I sit to you, I insist upon having a set-to with you.' Hayman, astonished at the oddity of the observation, affected not to understand his visitor, whereupon the Marquis exclaimed, 'I have been told that you are one of the last boxers of the school of Broughton, and I flatter myself not altogether deficient in the pugilistic art; but since I have been in Germany I have got out of practice, therefore I want a little trial of your skill.' Hayman pleaded age [he was in his fifties] and gout as obstacles to his consent. To the first the Marquis replied, 'There was very little difference between them; and to the second, that he considered exercise as a specific remedy,' adding, laughing, 'besides, a few rounds will cause a glow of countenance that will give animation to the canvass.' Hayman no longer resisted; the gloves were donned, and to it they went. After a good display of strength and science, Hayman delivered such a straight hit in the 'bread-basket', that down they both went with a tremendous crash. This brought up stairs the affrighted Mrs Hayman, who found the academician and commander-in-chief rolling over each other on the carpet like two unchained bears.

Whether it was the usual practice of Royal Academicians always to keep boxing gloves in their studios, or whether the noble Marquis brought his own on the offchance, is, unfortunately, not related.

If George Townshend is credited with being the earliest British caricaturist, far better known is James Gillray. In a hurriedly etched publication of 10 July 1788, just one day after the event depicted, Gillray presented the nineteen-year-old John Jackson in his first fight. 'Gentleman' Jackson is employing a favourite tactic of holding and hitting to demolish the huge Tom Fewtrell. At the ringside are to be seen those inveterate fight fanatics the Prince of Wales, the Duke of Hamilton, Lord Derby and Colonel Hanger, yet there is no evidence here of the usual grimacing and slobbering with

DUNN. WARD.   FUTRELL. JACKSON. JOHNSON. WYNDHAM.SMITH.HUMPHRE

which Gillray so often enhanced the features of his victims. Best known for his cruel political satires, the mocking element of his work is curiously absent from his depictions of prize-fight scenes, which he endowed with a seriousness amounting in at least one instance to grandeur. Gillray's superbly drawn etching of 1790, showing Mendoza in his third fight with Dick Humphries, is surely one of the noblest representations of the noble art in existence. This unexpected aspect of Gillray's work, together with the speed of production (ten days between fight and publication) may in part be explained by the similarity of the figure of Mendoza to a portrait of his adversary which had been published as a mezzotint two years earlier from a painting by John Hoppner.

Hoppner, who had worked for the Royal Family since 1785 and became a member of the Royal Academy in 1795, was generally much happier with pictures of women and children. However, in his portrait of Richard Humphries, the painter successfully conveys an impression of fortitude in the face, combined with latent violence and strength in the arms and torso of the bruiser. The power of these attributes is enhanced and heightened, in the best tradition of the Romantic Revival,

In this hastily produced etching, James Gillray illustrates the questionable tactics by which the future champion, John Jackson, won his first professional fight against Tom Fewtrell at Smitham Bottom, near Croydon, in 1788.

by the combination of a mountainous landscape and tempestuous sky in the background. This same formula was successfully followed by the French artist, Charles Jean Robineau, who in the same year used exactly the same ingredients but a different pose in his full-length portrait of Mendoza. It would be interesting to know who plagiarised whom?

A famous contemporary of Gillray and Hoppner was Thomas Rowlandson, who began his career as a painter of portraits and other serious subjects, but, having gambled away his considerable earnings, was forced to pay off his debts with an enormous output of drawings and prints in which he mocked the manners of Georgian society. He remains the most prolific depictor and derider of all aspects of English life, boxing included.

One of the earliest of Rowlandson's prize-fight scenes is an extremely lively watercolour of the fight between Richard Humphries and Sam Martin, 'The Bath Butcher', which took place at Newmarket in 1786. In a composition which captures all the atmosphere of this Mecca of flat-racing, the combatants, shadowed by their respective seconds, square up to each other in a ring formed of stout wooden poles and rails. The bottleholders wait eagerly for the fall which will signify the end of a round, while the posts in neutral corners are used to obtain a bird's eye view by two figures who appear to be umpires. Outside the ring occurs the mayhem usually associated with both prize-fighting and Rowlandson. A rustic fumbles in the skirts of a wench who is seated in a cart, her arm around a third party. Horses shy, an orange-seller drops her wares, and a fat women who has just been enjoying her lunch sprawls bare breasted as the vehicle on which she was recently perched is overturned, spilling the other occupants in every direction to the considerable amusement of the bystanders. A horseman wearing the Star of the Garter looks nonchalantly on. Could this be the Prince of Wales or the Duke of York? Both were present, accompanied by the Dukes of Orleans and De Fitzjames. Despite the attendance of royalty, the ring itself appears the safest place to be!

This prolific artist produced several other drawings and prints depicting prize-fights, including those between Warr and Quirk in 1806, and Dutch Sam and Medley in 1810. Perhaps the most extraordinary of all is a satire, published in 1792, entitled 'Six Stages of Marring a Face', in which we follow a pugilist through six frames, or rounds, by the last of which he is battered out of all recognition.

Similar in vein to the riotous Humphries *v.* Martin drawing is a delightful etching from the series 'Rural Sports', produced by Rowlandson twenty-five years later and depicting the end of the second fight between Cribb and Molineaux. The English Champion has just delivered a straight right to the throat of his adversary, who is in the act of falling. The dismay

As a counter-attraction to Hoppner's picture of Humphries, Charles Jean Robineau's portrait of Mendoza, 'The Most Scientific Boxer Ever Known', was, in turn, commissioned by the rival fighter's chief backer. This mezzotint by Henry Kingsbury was then published following Mendoza's initial defeat of Humphries in 1789.

of his second is as obvious as the delight of the crowd who shout and wave ecstatically, with the exception of a countryman in the right foreground, who is being bitten by a horse.

Most surprising of all the works inspired by this famous fight, which took place in 1811, is a stunning lithograph entitled 'Boxeurs', created by the young French genius Théodore Géricault, who was working in London between 1817 and 1819. 'Boxeurs' was drawn long before any Frenchman had learned to box, indeed Géricault was the first French artist to take an interest in any aspect of the English way of life. The artist had almost certainly seen a copy of *Boxiana*, the then recently republished first volume of which contained a fold-out engraving of the fight. Was he attracted to the subject matter, by the black boxer's French name, or by the interesting juxtaposition of colour and tone displayed by the skin of the protagonists? Géricault appears to have based the poses of his combatants on the frontispiece of *Boxiana*, which shows one of many engravings of Mendoza and Humphries. In contrast to the aggressively English gestures of the top-hatted Corinthian on the right of Géricault's composition, the spectator reclining to the left bears far more resemblance to an antique river deity, than to any member of the London fancy. The ropes and stakes are absent, as they would have been in ancient Olympia, and the only discordant notes in an otherwise purely classical composition are struck by the Corin-

Tom Cribb knocks out Molineaux at Thistleton Gap, in Thomas Rowlandson's etching from a series entitled Rural Sports.

'Boxeurs' by Theodore Géricault.
The poses adopted by the protagonists
in this extraordinary lithograph of
c1818, owe much to the frontispiece
of the then popular Boxiana.

thian's top hat and Cribb's stylish trousers, which come straight from the latest Regency fashion plate.

The classical poses adopted by the bare-knuckle fighters have come in for much criticism. On one hand it has been stated that from the evidence of the paintings and prints they simply did not know how to punch correctly. They 'all adopted the same stance: feet set too wide and too square to make full use of their height and weight. They squat down on their haunches, knees bent outwards, and, one must assume, stood foot-fast in a slugging match.' To counter this opinion it has been suggested that they stood in such stiff poses because blows were delivered and received from a more or less predictable angle, and certain throws were allowed. Therefore prize-fighters were guarding against a totally different method of attack from that experienced by any modern boxer. There is an element of truth in both of these assertions. Prize-fighting in the mid-eighteenth century had generally been a pretty static affair, as can be seen from Captain Godfrey's description of Jack Broughton, written in 1747:

> . . . he steps not back, distrusting of himself, to stop a blow,
> and piddle in the return, with an arm unaided by his body,

producing but a kind of fly-flap blows, such as pastrycooks use to beat those insects from their tarts and cheese-cakes. No! Broughton steps bold and firmly in, bids a welcome to the coming blow; receives it with his guardian arm; then, with a general summons of his swelling muscles, and his firm body seconding his arm, and supplying it with all its weight, pours the pile-driving force upon his man.

By the turn of the century Jem Belcher was moving rapidly around the ring, springing backwards and forwards, and throwing more punches from more angles than had hitherto been thought possible. Even the stolid Tom Cribb was famous for 'milling on the retreat', as 'back pedalling' whilst counter-punching was then termed, but the paintings and prints contemporary with these new departures lose little or none of their stiffness.

There is an interesting parallel in the depiction of race-horses which at this time were always shown galloping with legs thrown out fore and aft, all four hoofs coming off the ground at the same time. This was to be the formula for depicting horses and was accepted as being the way in which they always moved until the advent of photography in the mid-nineteenth century proved otherwise. The same is true of fighting men. They are shown in poses which are a formula, based upon the ritual 'setting to' with which all well regulated fights began. Added to this, certain antique overtones were introduced by artists steeped in classical sculpture. While this formalisation is to be seen in many examples of boxing art, it is certainly not present in them all: as we have seen, Rowland-son's drawing of Humphries and Martin, or Cribb and Molineaux were extremely lively portrails.

George Cruikshank protested that this drawing of him in a pugilistic pub, by his friend Daniel Maclise, showed him 'doing what I never did in the whole course of my life – that is, making a sketch of anyone'. However, we have Egan's testimony that whenever an interesting scene presented itself during their joint 'research' for Life in London, *'Cruiky booked it'.*

Cribb's triumph also inspired George Cruikshank to pro-duce a brutally realistic etching within days of the fight. In this etching, the disfigured Englishman is once again deliver-ing the *coup de grâce* to poor Molineaux, while Bill Richmond, the black boxer's black second, rolls his eyes in comic horror.

George Cruikshank, together with his brother Robert, was to be responsible for the illustrations to Pierce Egan's *Life in London,* of which, in later life, both brothers claimed, with varying justification, to be the inspiration and guiding genius. The 1821 best-seller is certainly remembered today, less for Egan's text than for the delightful plates in which we accom-pany the heroes, Tom, Jerry and Bob Logic, 'in their Rambles and Sprees through the Metropolis'. The Cruikshank brothers had accompanied Egan in his own 'rambles and sprees' gathering first-hand information for their joint production; in fact, the unlikely trio were widely believed, at the time, to have been the originals of the resulting books' main charac-ters. While the brothers can hardly be said to correspond to a pair of fashionable bucks, Egan, with his fondness for a 'bit of life' and unending fund of excruciating puns, did bear a strong resemblance to the Oxonian Bob Logic, and with his own scanty education would have been more than pleased to be mistaken for a university man, even, or perhaps especially an alcoholic one. Within the Cruikshank illustrations, we spend an afternoon with John Jackson at his sparring rooms in Bond Street, where Corinthian Tom puts on the gloves with Jackson, while Jerry is weighed for a bet. That evening we visit Tom Cribb's pub where our Corinthian friend, holding the Champion's Cup, introduces us to the ponderous ex-pug, at home in his cosy parlour. The room is lined with sporting prints, among which can be recognised portraits of both Jackson and John Gully.

Thackeray, looking back in respectable Victorian middle age to the good old 'Tom and Jerry days of his youth, when fistycuffs were the fashion', though disappointed by Egan's outmoded style of writing, was to exclaim, 'But the pictures! – Oh! The pictures are noble still!'

Before the advent of Tom and Jerry, Robert Cruikshank had produced an extraordinary comic strip, some thirteen feet long, by $3\frac{3}{8}$ inches deep, entitled 'The Fancy on the Road to Moulsey Hurst', with accompanying text by Egan. Depicted and described are representatives of all classes of Regency society, from the nobleman down to the occupants of a dust-cart, all jostling their way the fifteen-odd miles from the sporting pubs of the capital, via Hyde Park Corner turnpike, to the favourite venue of the prize-ring, situated on the south bank of the Thames, opposite Hampton.

Moulsey Hurst was famous as a site for cricket matches as well as prize-fights, and here, pencil in hand at ringside or pitch, could often be found that phenomenon peculiar to England in the eighteenth and nineteenth centuries – the sporting artist. That is, one who draws and paints sporting scenes and personalities to the total or partial exclusion of other subject-matter.

One of the most prolific sporting artists of the early nineteenth century was Ben Marshall. Best known for his painting of horses and hounds, Marshall also produced portraits in oil of some prize ring champions. At the Tate Gallery, elegantly dressed Jem Belcher is seen out walking in about 1803, the year in which he lost an eye while playing rackets, an event which was to end a brilliant run of successes in the ring. The twenty-two-year-old Belcher is wearing around his neck the fashionable silk handkerchief to which he gave his name.

John Jackson, also shown dressed in the height of fashion, stands full length and full square, his upturned top hat placed in an unfortunate position beneath the nude statue of an antique boxer. This powerful portrait was beautifully reproduced as a mezzotint by Charles Turner in about 1810, and

Byron probably referred to the large mezzotint by Charles Turner, after the painting by Ben Marshall, when, in 1813, he wrote to a friend concerning the whereabouts of 'Jack's graven image'.

has since appeared in engraved form, ranging from the skilful to the indifferent, in just about every illustrated history of boxing ever produced. It is even to be seen, minus the statue, embossed in gold onto the spines of the three volumes of *Pugilistica*.

Marshall made a happier choice of background material for his portrait of John Gully, in which the stylish ex-bruiser is complimented by a copy of the much admired group of Grecian pankratiasts from the Uffizi in Florence. One of the best copies of this famous marble carving was by the great neo-classical sculptor Antonio Canova, who later completed four figures of ancient pugilists, still to be seen in the Vatican. These masterly statues were to receive scant praise from Jon

Bee, who in the 1824 *Boxiana,* while grudgingly acknowledging the artist's skill, dismissed them with the critisicm: 'Whatever may be the merits of the chisel, so unbusiness-like are their attitudes, and so completely do they lay themselves open, that an English boy of sixteen would quickly dispose of them all.' That the artist was obviously not party to the inside knowledge reputedly enjoyed by his earlier compatriot Torrigiano, is apparent from Bee's chauvinistic closing remark: 'However, Canova, when he made these statues, had not had the benefit of a journey to London.'

To return to sporting artists, another celebrated contemporary of Marshall's was Henry Alken, who produced some plates dealing with the peripheral areas of the prize-ring in 1821, when later in the same year that had seen the publication of Egan's *Life in London,* an anonymous author cashed in with *Real Life in London.* Among the half-dozen artists who worked on what Egan called this 'bare faced piracy', Alken was responsible for 'A private turn up, in the drawing-room of a Noble Marquis.' There followed two plates depicting the road to a fight, which were blatantly modelled on Robert Cruikshank's previously published strip. A scene, set in the Fives Court, also bears more than a passing resemblance to Cruikshank's aquatint of the same subject. Unfortunately the rest of Alken's rather bland forays into the world of prize-fighting are, like these plagiarisms, not in the same class as his more familiar huntin', shootin' and fishin' scenes.

The Fives Court in St Martin's Lane was a favourite gathering place for all devotees of the prize-ring. Innumerable benefits and sparring exhibitions were held here between 1802 and 1826, when the area was demolished to make way for the Trafalgar Square development. Despite the productions of Alken and the Cruikshanks, by far the best representation of the Fives Court was created by the otherwise unknown C. Blake. In 1821 Charles Turner produced a superb etching based on Blake's painting, which shows the court packed to capacity with spectators, whilst a sparring match between Randall and Turner is in progress in the ring. In the foreground of this enormous work can be recognised the detailed portrait of almost every well-known fighter of the time, including Jem Belcher, who had been dead for many years before Randall and Turner ever sparred together. Some of these portraits are based upon the drawings of George Sharples, who was by far the most prolific delineator of the features of fighting men.

Working in the years around 1820, the ubiquitous Sharples drew the portraits of most leading pugilistis, many of which were then engraved for the pages of *Boxiana.* The circumstances surrounding Sharples' portrait of Dan Donnelly are particularly well documented. In the summer of 1819 Donnelly was in training at Riddlesdown near Croydon for his fight with Tom Oliver, and had just been liberally wined and dined by several gentlemen amateurs when he sat for his portrait. This was the famous occasion on which Donnelly was reprimanded for eating large quantities of green peas whilst in training, 'and sure is it a PAE that will hurt me; no! nor a drop of the cratur neither', exclaimed the Irish champion throwing back yet another large brandy. The portrait was '. . . pronounced by the company present to be a facsimile of the original. Donnelly himself was well pleased with the exertions of the artist on viewing his "own Mug", as he called it.'

Another artist who drew almost 'photographic' likenesses of prize-fighters was Thomas Wageman. Later to become portrait painter to the King of Holland, Wageman was already well known for his portraits of eminent actors and actresses when he stylishly sketched the likenesses of Tom Cannon and his successor as champion, Jem Ward.

In contrast to Sharples and Wageman, the fashionable Samuel Drummond did not draw boxers, nor indeed any sporting subjects at all. Known today for his portraits of Sir Marc Brunel and Elizabeth Fry, he confined his activities to the rich and famous; John Gully was emphatically in both these categories when Drummond portrayed him in fleshly middle age. Prize-ring champion back in 1807, the financial genius Gully was to become a successful bookmaker and racehorse owner; he also appears in Sir George Hayter's huge oil painting of the reformed parliament of 1833. In this immense picture, the ex-pug, now Honourable Member for Pontifract, is to be seen looking us in the eye from the gallery of the House of Commons. Immediately below, the Duke of Wellington presents a disdainful back to the 'shocking bad hats', who, like Mr Gully, have just been elected by the hitherto ignored industrial conurbations. Despite protests by the Iron Duke and his select circle, a new age was dawning.

The early 1820s, which had produced so much excellent work by the Cruikshanks and their contemporaries, may also be regarded as the beginning of the end to the marriage of fine art and the prize-ring. The two great contests between Spring and Langan in 1824 produced very few pictorial manifestations. Certainly none at all was of the quality inspired by the Cribb v. Molineaux epics of the previous generation. While not claiming actual greatness for much of the work that had gone before, it must be admitted that the art of the prize-ring went into steep decline at the same time as the ring itself, the reasons for which are not difficult to see.

After the mid 1820s pugilism had ceased to be a fashionable pursuit and the men of taste and influence who had once provided the backing for prize-fights began to drift away from an activity which was fast falling inextricably into disrepute. The breed of backer which replaced the Althorps and Windhams lacked both the means and the culture of their aristocra-

George Sharples drew this excellent portrait of Irish champion, Dan Donnelly, during the summer of 1819, but 'Sir Dan' had drunk himself to death long before the engraved likeness appeared in Boxiana *two years later.*

tic predecessors. In consequence, the work of first-class and society painters began to be replaced by the productions of a host of skilled or semi-skilled journeymen, whose work exhibits every degree of competence and incompetence. The charming, full-length portraits of Deaf Burke and Bendigo, engraved by Charles Hunt in 1839 and 1846 respectively, show the old rivals in romantic landscapes, every bit as classically posed as Mendoza and Humphries of fifty years earlier. Thoroughly delightful and competent though these well-known aquatints may be, the technique and draughtsmanship bear the unmistakable hallmarks of folk art, rather than fine art.

The mention of Deaf Burke in the context of fine art, recalls the curious fact that while on tour in America during the late 1830s, 'The Deaf Un' appeared on the New York stage in a series of 'classical attitudes'. This lucrative if bizarre performance was, as with most incidents connected with poor simple-

The somewhat self-indulgent features captured in Samuel Drummond's portrait of an affluent John Gully, belie a shrewd and forceful businessman.

REPRODUCED BY COURTESY OF THE NATIONAL PORTRAIT GALLERY, LONDON.

minded Burke, replete with unwitting humour. New York's playbills blazed forth the following inducement:

THE CHAMPION BOXER OF ENGLAND,
THE CELEBRATED AND HERCULEAN

DEAF BURKE

Mr Burke will make his first appearance as the Venetian Statue, which he will exhibit on a pedestal, with appropriate change of figure, attitude, and expression. The arrangement is made in order to convey to the classical taste of artists, in an efficient manner, a series of beautiful compositions of ancient sculpture. The following is the order of the portraitures—

(1) Hercules struggling with the Nemean lion, in five attitudes.
(2) Achilles throwing the discus or quoit, in two attitudes.
(3) The slave, Emoleur, the grinder, sharpening his knife whilst overhearing the conspirators.
(4) Two positions of the athletic combatants, as fighting gladiators.
(5) Samson slaying the Philistines with a jaw bone.
(6) The African alarmed at the thunder.
(7) Ajax defying the lightning.
(8) Romulus, from David's picture of the Sabines.
(9) Remus's defence from the same.
(10) Cain slaying his brother Abel.
(11) Samson lifting the gates of Gaza.
(12) The whole to conclude with the five celebrated positions of the dying gladiator.

We are informed by a facetious correspondent that a couple of years later, while on a trip to Paris in company with the Marquess of Waterford, Burke attempted to add the Venus de Medici to his repertoire, but that this was a decided failure.

On a more serious note, ex-champion Jem Ward took up painting as an accompaniment to the profession of publican, upon retirement from active combat in 1832. His work, which was a competent example of the naïve school, was hung at the Liverpool Exhibition on several occasions during the old champion's residence in that city. Among other good notices received from the journals of the time, one critic was to write: 'Had Ward devoted himself to the study and practice of painting in his earlier years, he would doubtless have attained eminence.' Henry Downes Miles, the author of *Pugilistica,* was certainly impressed when visiting Jem's studio. He was particularly taken with some seascapes, 'which bore marks of peculier talent and no mean skill of manipulation'.

When Sayers fought Heenen in 1860, old Jem was on hand

to produce a lively drawing of the proceedings, from which engravings were later sold as souvenirs of the event. Whether or not the artist realised any profit from the venture is not known, but Miles had earlier warned that: 'Ward's hobbies, painting and music, adopted late in life, we fear injured his wordly calling as a sporting boniface, and, after several failures, he retired . . . into that admirable institution, The Licensed Victuallers' Asylum, in the Old Kent Road.' Participation in the fine arts by a professional boxer, seems to have excited the same degree of disapprobation from the Victorian fancy, as the awful discovery that one of Jem's modern counterparts once actually read a book!

The English way of life had changed beyond recognition during the 1830s and 1840s. Royal Academicians who portrayed the new young Queen had long since ceased to spar with popular bruisers, and the better cartoonists became far more genteel than the Rowlandsons and Gillrays of the previous robust era. In a new climate of respectability which was to permeate the Victorian age, it would be as hard to imagine Millais or Tenniel chatting to 'The Tipton Slasher' at ringside as Prince Albert himself.

This lithograph of Tom Sayers, by the American printers Currier & Ives, was taken from a photograph published in London by George Newbold.

By mid-century, the advent and spread of photography was to help remove as much spontaneity and freshness from what remained of prize-ring art as it had taken from art in general. When we look at the otherwise splendid lithographic portrait of Tom Sayers, published by George Newbold immediately prior to the great fight with Heenan, we are forcibly struck with the resemblance to one of Newbold's stiffly posed photographs taken with an achingly long exposure.

The Sayers and Heenen fight of 1860 probably produced more paintings, engravings, lithographs and general ephemera than any one sporting event before or since. Ranging in execution from the competent to the downright hamfisted, these charming memorabilia in no instance ever reach the level of achievement of works by the likes of Rowlandson and Géricault, commemorating that great international fight of half a century earlier.

Cribb had fought Molineaux in the old, pre-photographic, rural England, in the days of stagecoaches and highwaymen, a vanished world in which Pierce Egan, 'The Thucydides of the Ring', had once exclaimed:

Nature seemed to have provided these milling smiths with good, solid, substantial and effective sledge hammers, with which they milled the nobs, breasts, ribs and loins of each other in the heartiest good humour . . . The English claret had flowed so freely that never before or since did I see two men so thoroughly and handsomely painted with the true blood red, from the crown of the head to the waistband. They would have made a rare subject for a painter.

CHAPTER 3

WRITERS AND THE RING

The Chicken . . . had the misfortune to get into Chancery early in the proceedings when he was severely fibbed by the Larky one, and heavily grassed. But it appeared from the published records of that great contest that the Larky Boy had had it all his own way from the beginning, and that the Chicken had been tapped, and bunged, and had received pepper, and had been made groggy, and had come up piping, and had endured a complication of similar strange inconveniences, until he had been gone into and finished.

CHARLES DICKENS, *DOMBEY AND SON*, 1844–6

In this illustration by 'Phiz' to Dombey & Son, Charles Dickens' *drunken pug 'The Game Chicken' pays a visit to Uncle Sol's shop, to the evident delight of the young assistant who thus 'had the honour of staring for nearly half an hour at the conqueror of the Nobby Shropshire One'.*

The downfall of Dickens' uncouth and boozy pug, 'The Game Chicken', is here burlesqued in the style of *Bell's Life*, the premier early Victorian sporting journal. Clearly *Bell's* fight reports were familiar to the creator of *Dombey*, who expected his readers to understand the allusion and to share his joke.

Born in 1812, the year which saw the initial publication of *Boxiana* in celebration of Tom Cribb's second triumph over Molineaux, young Charles Dickens had grown up in and around London at a time when the craze for pugilism was at its height. By the time of *Dombey and Son*, the popularity of prize-fighting was well into its decline, although some important matches still continued to attract huge crowds. The socially concerned Dickens disapproved most strongly of what he saw as a squalid leftover from an immoral era, but the prize-ring and its adherents, as integral if unwanted components of the current English scene, could not fail to find a place in his writing.

If Dickens perceived pugilism from the standpoint of emergent Victorian respectability, writers of an earlier age had viewed the phenomenon quite differently. The reactions of Georgian authors had ranged from an amused, live-and-let-live approach to a full-blown approval for what they considered an essentially English and morally uplifting practice.

As early as 1725, Dr John Byrom, more famous perhaps as the author of 'Christians Awake! Salute the happy morn', had written 'Extempor Verses upon a Trial of Skill between the Two Great Masters of the Noble Science of Defence, Messrs Figg and Sutton'. These amusing verses concluded with some disparaging classical comparisons, very apt in an era of Palladian country villas and 'Rule Britannia':

Now after such Men, who can bear to be told
Of your Roman and Greek puny Heroes of old?
To compare such poor Dogs as Alcides and Theseus
To Sutton and Figg would be very facetious.
Were Hector himself, with Apollo to back him,
To encounter with Sutton, – zooks, how he would thwack him!

Although Byrom elsewhere describes his protagonists as prize-fighters, the trial of skill is one in which back-sword and quarterstaff are employed, in preference to the newly emergent bare fist.

The term prize-fighter had been used by writers as diverse as Samuel Pepys in the mid-seventeenth century and Dr Johnson a hundred years later to describe not just boxers, but anyone who fought for a prize, with or without swords or other potentially lethal weapons. In 1662 Pepys had attended one such prize-fight and noted with apparent glee that both contestants were 'cut several times both in head and legs . . . all over blood'. In the century which followed Pepys, few if any among the intelligentisia had expressed repugnance either moral or physical at this form of entertainment, any more than at ancient reports of gladiatorial combats, to which, barring the actual death of one or other of the competitors, prize-fighting with sharp weapons bore a strong resemblance.

By the middle years of the eighteenth century the practice of boxing with the bare fist had largely superseded the use of weapons in the provision of a popular spectacle. This movement towards a less deadly type of public combat coincided with the emergence, at least among the literati, of a new sensibility and regard for human life, which later in the century would be further propagated by revolutionary, egalitarian and romantic ideals.

One of the earliest writers to recognise the relatively humanitarian possibilities of a boxing match was Henry Fielding, who, in the pages of *Tom Jones*, first published in 1749, expressed a charmingly pacifist opinion most worthy of the Age of Reason:

We cannot suppress a pious wish, that all quarrels were to be decided by those weapons only which Nature, knowing what is proper for us, hath supplied; and that cold iron was to be used in digging no bowels but those of the earth, then would war, the pastime of the monarchs, be almost inoffensive, and battles between great armies might be fought at the particular desire of several ladies of quality, who, together with the kings themselves, might be the actual spectators of the conflict. Then might the field be this moment strewed with the dead bodies, and the next, the dead men might get up and fight, like Mr Bayes's troups, and march off, either at the sound of drum or fiddle, as should be previously agreed on. I would avoid, if possible, treating this matter ludicrously, lest grave men should be angry, and politicians, whom I know to be offended at a jest, might cry pish! at it; but in reality might not a battle be as well decided by the greater number of broken heads, bloody noses, and black eyes, as by the greater heap of mangled bodies.

Besides suggesting these rather unlikely military possibilities, Fielding, the earliest English writer specifically to mention contemporary pugilism, was not slow to appreciate the narrative and comic potential of what had by now become a highly fashionable exercise. Like many other young gentlemen in the time of George II, the lusty Tom Jones had the opportunity to demonstrate his fistic attainments on more than one occasion. Here he is attacked by a bullying footman, who delivers:

> . . . one of those punches in the guts, which, tho' the spectators at Broughton's Amphitheatre have such exquisite delight in seeing them, convey but very little pleasure in the feeling . . .

Jones, however, fought back heartily and soon overcame his antagonist, who:

> . . . having now recovered his legs, shook his head at Jones, and with a sagacious look, cry'd – 'O d-n me, I'll have nothing more to do with you, you have been upon the stage, or I am d-nably mistaken': and indeed we may forgive this his suspicion; for such was the agility and strength of our heroe, that he was perhaps a match for one of the first rate boxers, and could, with great ease, have beaten all the muffled graduates of Mr Broughton's school.

To explain the term 'muffled graduates', Fielding appended a footnote which quotes in full Jack Broughton's advertisement of 1747. Earlier in *Tom Jones,* the author had already evinced knowledge of what he is the first to call the 'noble art', when, in a passage which clearly proves boxing to have been a popular pursuit at English seats of learning in the early eighteenth century, he describes an impromptu bout between Jones and his redoubtable tutor, the Reverend Dr Thwackham. The good doctor, 'had been a champion in his youth, and had gained much honour by his fist, both at school and at the university'. Notwithstanding the doctor's credentials, youth will be served, and, following an amusing episode in which 'Many lusty blows, much more pleasant, as well as easy to have seen, than to read or describe, were given on both sides,' Tom again emerged victorious.

Fielding's contemporary, Dr Johnson, who physically and temperamentally bore more than a passing resemblance to Thwackham, was as pugnacious as the schools and universities could have wished. The ponderous lexicographer, whose uncle was reputed to have run a Smithfield cudgelling booth in the days of Figg, allegedly demonstrated a knowledge of the art when he not only knocked down an impudent bookseller in Covent Garden, but thrashed a vicious drayman in Fleet Street. The degree of truth contained in stories of this nature, where respectable public figures engage in street fights, is of little importance. The fact that reports of such incidents circulated in print, were widely believed and thoroughly approved of by a considerable section of the literate public serves to illustrate the prevailing attitude to such displays of blunt physical violence.

The equally belligerent William Cobbett was, as one would expect, a great believer in the advantages, both personal and national, to be gained from the practice and example of boxing. Writing in his *Political Register* in 1805, Cobbett refutes the cries of brutality which already, in the same year as the indescribable carnage of Trafalgar, were being directed towards pugilism, arguing that:

> ... of all the ways in which violence can possibly be committed ... none is so seldom fatal to the parties, as boxing ... This mode, by excluding the aid of everything extraneous, by allowing of no weapons, by leaving nothing to deceit, and very little to art of any sort, is, in most cases, decisive as to the powers of the combatants, and proceeds, besides, upon the generous principle that, with the battle, ceases for ever the cause whence it arose; a principle of such long and steady growth, so deeply rooted in the hearts of Englishmen, that to attempt to the revival, or even to allude to, with apparent resentment, the grounds of a quarrel which has been terminated by the fists is always regarded as a mark of baseness, whether visible in the conduct of the parties themselves, or in that of their relations or friends. As sports or exercises approach nearer and nearer to real combats, the greater, in spite of all we can say, is our admiration of those who therein excel. Belcher has, by the sons of cant, in every class of life, been held up to us as a monster, a perfect ruffian; yet there are very few persons who would not wish to see Belcher; few from whom marks of admiration have not, at some time, been extorted by his combats; and scarcely a female Saint, perhaps, who would not, in her way to the conventicle, or even during the snuffling there to be heard, take a peep at him from beneath her hood. Can as much be said by any one of those

noblemen and gentlemen who have been spending the best years of their lives in dancing by night and playing at cricket by day? The reason is, not that Belcher strikes hard; not that he is strong; not that he is an adept at his art; but that he exposes himself voluntarily to so much danger, and that he bears so many heavy blows.

While perhaps expressing the spirit of an age, we may assume from his comment about the absence of art in boxing that Cobbett had *not* seen Belcher.

Two years later, the poet Robert Southey, writing under the pseudonym of 'Don Manuel Alvarez Espriella' in his *Letters from England*, was to cite the English delight in pugilism as one of the many proofs of national barbarity, along with the eating of raw beef while in training. He continues: 'When the combat at length takes place, a regular report is prepared for the newspapers as if it were a national victory – the particulars are recorded with a minuteness at once ridiculous and disgraceful; for every movement has its technical or slang name, and the unprecedented science of the successful combatant becomes the theme of general admiration.' Southey concludes his spoof commentary upon the national pastime and incidentally shows his true colours by conceding that:

> . . .in England a boxing match settles all disputes among the lower classes, and when it is over they shake hands, and are friends. Another equally beneficial effect is the security afforded to the weaker by the laws of honour, which forbid all undue advantages; the man who should aim a blow below the waist, who should kick his antagonist, strike him when he is down, or attempt to injure him after he has yielded, would be sure to experience the resentment of the mob, who on such occasions always assemble to see what they call fair play, which they enforce as rigidly as the Knights of the Round Table did the laws of chivalry.

Other well-known literary figures from pugilism's golden age were not content merely to recommend the virtues of boxing; they pulled on the muffles and took lessons from one of the 'professors' who ran sparring academies. Within a year of Cobbett's spirited defence of the exercise, Lord Byron, while still in his teens, began to attend major prize-fights, and to spar with John Jackson. The friendship that developed between the poet and the pug was to last until 1816, in which year Byron left England forever.

As early as 1808, the young Lord had begun to correspond with his unusually literate boxing master about such matters as the wisdom of backing Dan Dogherty against the younger Belcher for a forthcoming contest which Dogherty, and by implication Byron, was to lose. Not to be discouraged, the

Overleaf: *Lord Byron decorated his famous dressing screen between 1812, the date of the most recent engraving contained in the montage, and 1816, the year in which he finally took leave of England.*

In a letter dated 12 June 1830, Pierce Egan, as ever trying to raise funds, wrote to a theatrical manager stating the screen to be in his possession: '. . . a splendid screen . . . made for the late Lord Byron and once valued at 200 guineas by his Lordship. The screen not only contains some valuable drawings by the late Rowlandson, but in other respects will be found highly interesting to a gentleman like yourself, fond of anything which exhibits talent.'

REPRODUCED BY COURTESY OF JOHN MURRAY LTD.

poet was, within a month, among the party of Corinthians at ringside to witness John Gully beating Bob Gregson for the Championship of England. What sum of money the embrionic fight patron won or lost on this occasion is not related, but Gregson seems to have backed himself heavily. Consequently, a mutual friend was soon to apply to Byron for 'certain paltry pounds sterling' to secure the release of the defeated pugilist from debtors' prison, a petition with which the poet was more than ready to assist.

Byron had been accepted as a regular member of the fancy, and was to be seen at pugilistic gatherings in company with leading members of the fraternity. In 1813, the now famous author of *Childe Harold* was to record one such occasion in his diary, and, incidentally, to supply an intimate picture of the newly retired Tom Cribb:

> Just returned from dinner with Jackson (the Emperor of Pugilism) and another of the select, at Cribb's the champion's. I drank more than I like, and have brought away some three bottles of very fair claret – for I have no headache. We had Tom up after dinner; – very facetious, though somewhat prolix. He don't like his situation – wants to fight again – pray Pollux (or Castor, if he was the miller) he may! Tom has been a sailor – a coal-heaver – and some other genteel profession, before he took to the cestus. Tom has been in action at sea, and is now only three-and-thirty. A great man! has a wife and a mistress, and conversations well – barring some sad omissions and misapplications of the aspirate. Tom is an old friend of mine; I have seen some of his best battles in my nonage. He is now a publican, and, I fear, a sinner.

A few months later, following a short lapse in his regular exercise, we find the poet writing to a friend:

> I have been sparring with Jackson for exercise this morning, and mean to continue and renew my acquaintance with my muffles. My chest and arms, and wind are in very good plight, and I am not in flesh. I used to be a hard hitter, and my arms are very long for my height (5 feet 8¼ inches); at any rate exercise is good, and this the severest of all; fencing and the broad-sword never fatigued me half so much.

Byron was hooked. According to Egan he even boxed in an attempt to raise his spirits on the morning of his own mother's funeral. He continued to write letters alluding to his sparring during the spring and summer of 1814, the year in which he became a member of the newly formed Pugilistic Club.

Byron, in many ways, epitomised the Regency buck with his predilections for pugilism, alcohol and pretty women, and

two of these diversions receive surprising attention in the design and decoration of a dressing-screen assembled by the poet at about this time. One side of the screen is covered with portraits of famous actresses of the time, while the other is literally smothered with cut-out engravings of pugilists, ranging in date from early Georgian James Figg to the contemporary Cribb and Molineaux. A prominent position on the screen is allotted to John Jackson himself, who must have seen and approved of the selection.

Later, during his self-enforced exile from England, Byron was often to write affectionately about his old teacher. There is even a note on the manuscript of *Don Juan* in which, having completed a verse containing several 'flash' terms, the poet adds: 'If there be any gemman so ignorant as to require a traduction, I refer him to my old friend and corporeal pastor and master, John Jackson, Esquire, professor of pugilism; who, I trust, still retains the strength and symmetry of his model of a form, together with his good humour, and athletic as well as mental accomplishments.'

Lord Byron spars with John Jackson in an illustration by Pierce Egan Junior, for his father's Every Gentleman's Manual. *Byron is transformed from the Cruikshanks' Corinthian Tom, by the simple addition of a Turkish Pelise, in which the poet sometimes boxed 'to prevent obesity'.*

Byron was to die in 1824 at the age of thirty-six while fighting in the cause of Greek nationalism. Ironically, his death took place in the year which marked the virtual end of pugilism's golden age with the retirement of Tom Spring and the closure, after almost thirty years, of John Jackson's Bond Street sparring-rooms.

> Boxer Byron
> Made of Iron, alias
> Boxiron

This inconsequential rhyme was followed a few pages later by the equally irrelevant words 'Jack Randall's challenge to All the World' scrawled into a notebook kept by the poet John Clare, when in his later years he was confined within a mental asylum. Byron and Randall were just two of the characters who Clare, in moments of insanity, imagined himself to be. He also believed he was, by turns, the fighters Tom Spring, Ben Caunt and Harry Jones, shadows from an earlier, happier period of his tragic life.

The newly famous and sportily dressed poet first visited London in the early 1820s, and while out walking with the sombrely attired Charles Lamb had provoked shouts of 'Tom and Jerry – there goes Tom and Jerry!' Like Jerry, the fashionable young provincial of Egan's best-seller, Clare had been taken to the Fives Court, and had watched the sparring with keen interest. He was particularly impressed by the appearance and skill of Harry Jones, whom he considered the 'finest fellow in the ring'. During his stay in the capital, Clare had also visited 'The Hole in the Wall' in Chancery Lane, then under the management of the terrific Jack Randall. The impressionable poet had later dreaded passing Randall's house alone, for fear of its influence upon his decision whether to devote himself to his muse or throw himself wholeheartedly into the pleasures of the fancy. Luckily for posterity, but perhaps sadly for Clare, he chose poetry.

The essayist William Hazlitt, who took boxing lessons from Bill Richmond, dreaded Randall's pub for a far more tangible reason, having once been threatened by mine host, 'when the conqueror of thirteen battles was more full of *blue ruin* than of good manners'. The 'Hole in the Wall' was, however, the starting point from which in December 1821 Hazlitt set out on his overnight journey for Hungerford Downs, via Newbury to see his first prize-fight:

> Reader, have you ever seen a fight? If not, you have a pleasure to come, at least if it is a fight like that between the Gas-man and Bill Neat. The crowd was very great when we arrived on the spot; open carriages were coming up, with streamers flying and music playing, and the country people

were pouring in over hedge and ditch in all directions . . .
About two hundred thousand pounds were pending.

So Hazlitt sets the scene for his classic description of a classic
occasion in the annals of pugilism. We travel down with
Thurtell, the fight-promoter and future celebrated murderer,
thinly disguised as Tom Turtle, hear anecdotes of Richmond,
Belcher, Broughton, Stevenson and Gully, and see Randall,
Turner and Scroggins pass on top of a coach. Hazlitt describes
the actual fight and the downfall of the hitherto invincible
Gasman with a fascinated horror, which, together with his
word-picture of the surrounding scene, makes 'The Fight' one
of the great works of sporting prose. When afterwards our
guide asks Tom Cribb if he did not think the contest a good
one, and the old champion replies 'pretty well', we can but
concur with his sentiments, it was 'The Complete Thing'.

Three years before Hazlitt's outing, John Keats, perhaps
the most unlikely literary figure to have ever been seen at
ringside, was present at Crawley Down to witness the epic
battle between Randall and Ned Turner, which lasted for two
hours and nineteen minutes before the latter collapsed
through exhaustion. It appears that the poet's brother considered a sixty-mile round trip, punctuated by a two-hour
blood-bath in December, just the thing to cheer up a melancholy consumptive, following the death of his father.

One of the party on this occasion was almost certainly
Keats' friend, the poet, lawyer, gambler and fight-follower
John Hamilton Reynolds. Borrowing his *nom de plume* 'Peter
Corcoran' from an eighteenth-century Irish bruiser, Reynolds
was at the time engaged in the preparation of a collection of
poems entitled 'The Fancy'. Contained in this extraordinary
compilation of verse are several pugilistic pieces, including a
sonnet to Jack Randall, which is probably the best of many
written in praise of that invincible boxer:

*The crude but powerful Bill Neat,
hero of Hazlitt's* The Fight, *as
portrayed in a steel engraving by
Percy Roberts, after a drawing by
Read in* Bee's Boxiana *of 1824.*

> With marble-coloured shoulders and keen eyes
>   Protected by a forehead broad and white,
> And hair cut close lest it impede the sight,
>   And clenched hands, firm, and of punishing size,
> Steadily held, or motion'd wary-wise,
>   To hit or stop – and 'kerchief drawn too tight
> O'er the unyielding loins to keep from flight
>   The inconstant wind that all too often flies –
> The Nonpareil stands. Fame whose bright eyes run o'er
>   With joy to see a chicken of her own,
> Dips her rich pen in 'claret' and writes down
>   Under the letter 'R', first on the score,
> 'Randall, John – Irish parents – age not known–
>   Good with both hands, and only ten stone four.'

Obverse of a medal commemorating the fight between Bill Neat and Tom Hickman, 'The Gasman'. This brutal fight took place on Hungerford Downs on 12 December 1821 and was won by Neat after just twenty-three bloody minutes.

Reynolds was less enthusiastic about Phil Sampson, 'The Brummagem Youth', when, following the defeat of that boastful boxer by Aby Belasco, a clever Jewish lightweight, in February 1820, he advised:

Go back to Brummagem! go back to Brummagem!
  Youth of that ancient and halfpenny town!
Maul manufacturers; rattle, and rummage 'em;–
  Country swell'd heads may afford you renoun:
Here in Town-rings, we find Fame very fast go,
  The exquisite *light weights* are heavy to bruise;
For the graceful and punishing hand of Belasco
  Foils, – and *will* foil all attempts on the Jews.
      •   •   •
Turn up the raws at a fair or a holiday,
  Make your fist free with each Brummagem rib;
But never again, Lad, commit such a folly, pray!
  As sigh to be one of the messmates of Crib.
Leave the P.C. purse, for others to handle,–
  Throw up no hat in a Moulsey Hurst sun;–
Bid adieu, by the two-penny post, to Jack Randall,
  And take the outside of the coach, – one pound one!

Samson! forget there are such men as Scroggins,
  And Shelton and Carter, and Bob Burns and Spring:
Forget *toss for sides*, and forget all the floggings,–
  While shirts are pull'd off, – to make perfect the ring.
Your heart is a real one, but skill, Phil, is wanted;
  Without it, all uselessly bravery begs:–
Be content that you've beat Dolly Smith, and been *chaunted*,–
  And train'd, – stripp'd, – and pitted, – and hit off your legs!

Six months after his defeat by Belasco, Sampson was to lose again, this time to Jack Martin, Egan's 'Master of the Rolls'. In the pages of *Lavengro*, George Borrow tells us that early in his youth he had witnessed this fight, which took place near his native Norwich, together with a second contest between local heavy Ned Painter and Londoner, Tom Oliver. Writing in middle age, Borrow uses the occasion to launch into one of his many nostalgic eulogies of Old England:

Overleaf: George Sharples' portraits *of some of the bruisers featured in* Lavengro, *had been published in* Boxiana. *Anti-clockwise from top left they are: Shelton, Hudson, Randall, Spring, Turner and Scroggins.*

But those . . . were the days of pugilism; it was then at its height, and consequently near its decline, for corruption had crept into the ring . . . But what a bold and vigorous aspect pugilism wore at that time! and the great battle was just then coming off: the day had been decided upon, and the spot – a convenient distance from the old town; and to the old town were now flocking the bruisers of England, men of tremendous renown. Let no one sneer at the bruisers of England – what were the gladiators of Rome, or the

63

bull-fighters of Spain, in its palmiest days, compared to England's bruisers? . . . There they come, the bruisers, from far London, or from wherever else they might chance to be at the time, to the great rendezvous in the old city; some came one way, some another; some of tip-top reputation came with peers in their chariots, for glory and fame are such fair things, that even peers are proud to have those invested therewith by their sides; others came in their own gigs, driving their own bits of blood . . . I think I now see them, . . . the men of renown, amidst hundreds of people with no renown at all, who gaze upon them with timid wonder . . . There's Cribb, the champion of England, and perhaps the best man in England; there he is, with his huge massive figure, and face wonderfully like that of a lion. There is Belcher, the younger, not the mighty one, who is gone to his place, but the Teucer Belcher, the most scientific pugilist that ever entered a ring, only wanting strength to be, I won't say what. He appears to walk before me now, as he did that evening, with his white hat, white great coat, thin genteel figure, springy step, and keen, determined eye. Crosses him, what a contrast! grim, savage Shelton, who has a civil word for nobody, and a hard blow for anybody – hard! one blow, given with the proper play of his athletic arm, will unsense a giant. Yonder individual, who strolls about with his hands behind him, supporting his brown coat lappets, under-sized, and who looks anything but what he is, is the king of the light weights, so called – Randall! the terrible Randall, who has Irish blood in his veins; not the better for that, nor the worse; and not far from him is his last antagonist, Ned Turner, who, though beaten by him, still thinks himself as good a man, in which he is, perhaps, right, for it was a near thing; and 'a better shentleman', in which he is quite right, for he is a Welshman. But how shall I name them all? they were there by dozens, and all tremendous in their way. There was Bulldog Hudson, and fearless Scroggins, who beat the conqueror of Sam the Jew. There was Black Richmond – no, he was not there, but I knew him well; he was the most dangerous of blacks, even with a broken thigh. There was Purcell, who could never conquer till all seemed over with him. There was – what! shall I name thee last? ay, why not? I believe that thou art the last of all that strong family still above the sod, where mayst thou long continue – true species of English stuff, Tom of Bedford – sharp as Winter, kind as Spring.

Stirring stuff, even if the writer has fallen into the Hibernian habit, introduced by Egan and the Dowlings, of ascribing Irish parentage to Jack Randall, who always strongly denied the assertion. Borrow, for reasons not quite clear, also calls Herefordshire-born-and-bred Tom Spring, 'Tom of Bedford'.

It is, however, patently true that pugilism was near its decline.

Writing in the early 1830s, of events which had by then become all too common, the popular novelist, William Harrison Ainsworth, has one of the characters in *Rookwood* recite the following verses, entitled 'The Double Cross, which were 'trolled forth after a maudlin manner,' as well they might be:

Though all of us have heard of *crost* fights;
And certain *gains,* by certain *lost* fights;
I rather fancies that it's news,
How in a mill, *both* men should *lose*;
For vere the *odds* are thus made *even,*
It plays the dickens with the *steven*;
Besides, against all rule they're sinning,
Vere *neither* has *no* chance of vinning.

Two *milling* coves, each vide avake,
Vere backed to fight for heavy stake:
But in the meantime, so it vos,
Both *kids* agreed to *play a cross*;
Bold came cach *buffer* to the *scratch,*
To make it look a *tightish match*;
They *peeled* in style, and bets were making,
'Tvos six to four, but few were *taking*.

Quite cautiously the mill began,
For neither knew the other's plan;
Each *cull* completely in the *dark,*
Of vot might be his neighbour's *mark*;
Resolved his *fibbing* not to mind,
Nor yet to *pay him back in kind*;
So on each other *kept they tout*,
And *sparred* a bit, and *dodged* about.

Vith *mawleys* raised, Tom bent his back,
As if to plant a heavy thwack:
Vile Jem, vith neat left-handed *stopper,*
Straight threatened Tommy with *a topper*;
'Tis all my eye! no claret flows,
No *facers* sound—no smashing blows—
Five minutes pass, yet not a *hit,*
How can it end, pals?—vait a bit.

Each cove vos *teazed* with double duty,
To please his backers, yet *play booty*;
Ven, luckily for Jem, a *teller*
Vos planted right upon his *smeller*;
Down dropped he, stunned; ven time was called,
Seconds in vain the *seconds* bawled;
The *mill* is o'er, the crosser *crost,*
The *loser's von,* the vinner's *lost*!

It was at about this time that Ainsworth introduced the young Charles Dickens to his first publisher. Dickens had, up to this period, been working as a parliamentary reporter in which capacity he had written a description of Mr Gully, the honourable member for Pontifract:

> The quiet gentlemanly-looking man in the blue surtout, grey trousers, white neckerchief and gloves, whose closely buttoned coat displays his manly figure and broad chest to advantage, is a very well known character. He had fought a great many battles in his time and conquered, like the heroes of old, with no other arms than those the gods gave him.

A few years later Dickens presents a new insight into the short political career of John Gully when in the pages of *Nicholas Nickleby* the ex-pug makes an appearance, thinly disguised as the overbearing and self-opinionated MP, Mr Gregsbury. Dickens has the largely autobiographical Nicholas apply for the post of personal secretary to Gregsbury, whose name, it will be noticed, bears a strong resemblance to that of Gregson, the pugilistic victim of Gully from that gentleman's pre-parliamentary youth.

The interview between Gregsbury and the hopeful applicant is interrupted by a highly dissatisfied deputation from the MP's constituency, led by the appropriately named Mr Pugstyles. These puglistic surnames, together with the belligerent character of the self-made MP, strongly suggest that the youthful Dickens had actually been interviewed by the rich and successful ex-bruiser. The young writer seems to have come away from the meeting with a far less agreeable opinion of the old fighter than that which his prepossessing appearance, from a distance, had led him to expect.

In the pages of *Nicholas Nickleby*, which Dickens was at some pains not to have compared to Egan's *Life in London*, the young author also expresses contempt for the Corinthian followers of pugilism with his satirical portrait of the vicious profligate and roué, Sir Mulberry Hawke, who, in a brawl worthy of Tom and Jerry, is badly beaten by Nicholas, despite having been, in his younger days, 'a patron of the ring'.

Dombey and Son, published in the mid-1840s, introduces Mr Toots, a prize-ring patron of a very different nature to that of Sir Mulberry. Toots is a feeble-minded, but good-natured, young gentleman who, upon coming into his considerable inheritance, promptly:

> . . . devoted himself to the cultivation of those gentle arts which refine and humanise existence, his chief instructor in which was an interesting character called the Game Chicken, who was always to be heard of at the bar of the Black

Mercy! what a din and clatter,
  Breaks the stillness of the night,
Lamps do rattle,---'tis a battle,
  Quick, and let us see the sight.
Old and young at blows like fury,
  Tom and Jerry leads the row,
Milling, flooring all before them,
  This is Life in London, boys.

Badger, wore a shaggy white great-coat in the warmest weather, and knocked Mr Toots about the head three times a week, for the small consideration of ten and six per visit.

The Game Chicken subsequently makes many more-or-less comic appearances in company with Mr Toots, and we are informed that besides the shaggy white great-coat, the Chicken's most prominent features consisted of a flat-brimmed hat, very short hair and a head and nose both of which 'had been many times broken, and but indifferently repaired'. Dickens makes a great deal of fun with this pugilistic character and the language of the prize-ring throughout *Dombey and Son,* in which as we have seen he draws heavily on *Bell's Life* and *Boxiana* for models. He even appropriates the ring name of the factual but deceased Henry Pearce and bestows it upon Mr Toots' protégé.

George Bernard Shaw has written convincingly about the incredibility of what he calls Dickens' pious attempt to caricature a prizefighter, and the boorish Chicken certainly does not possess the professional ability of his namesake, nor the polish of John Jackson. But, bearing in mind the greater writer's familiarity with *Bell's Life,* it is just possible to see in the Game Chicken something of the character of his contemporary 'Deaf Burke', and perhaps it is not too fanciful to recognise shades of Bendigo in the Chicken's nemesis, 'The Larky Boy'.

In addition to *Dombey* and *Nicholas Nickleby,* several other Dickensian classics, including *The Pickwick Papers, Oliver Twist* and *Great Expectations,* contain much pugilistic allusion and metaphor. This in itself implies no love of the noble art; indeed Dickens was never a sportsman of any kind, but it does serve to demonstrate the depth to which the tastes of an earlier age had penetrated the most popular examples of early Victorian literature. Taken together with the author's copious use of sporting and lower-class slang, it also suggests that he owed rather more to the literary productions of Pierce Egan than he was willing to admit.

If the best loved English novelist ever actually attended a prize-fight, he has left us no record of the occasion. He has, however, been accused, along with Thackeray and almost every other literary and non-literary figure both living and dead, of being present at the great international contest in 1860 between Sayers and Heenan. In fact Dickens deputed journalist John Hollingshead to cover the event for his newly founded periodical, *All the Year Round.* Any confusion as to the authorship of the resulting report has probably arisen from the unmistakably Dickensian tone which it bears:

When I went out into the frosty air, instead of going comfortably to bed, about one o'clock A.M., on Tuesday

Now Jerry's become a Fancy blade,
To Jacksons he often goes,
And to shew his skill in the milling trade,
He crack'd poor Logick's nose.
He gloried in having a turn-up,
And was always the first in a lark,
To bang and wallop the Charlies,
And pommil them in the dark.

These crude wood-engraved copies of the Cruikshank brothers' illustrations are part of a cheap broadsheet edition of Life in London. *Published by James Catnach within weeks of Egan's bestseller, the accompanying verses continued to encourage fashionable young men to behave in a far from sporting manner towards 'Charlies', as night-watchmen were then known.*

morning, the seventeenth of April, I held a railway-ticket in my hand . . . A Journey from London-bridge to nowhere and back, by a special four o'clock train was all that I was guaranteed by this slip of cardboard, in return for the sum of three pounds sterling. For all this seeming mystery, the railway company knew that I was going to the great prize fight; the policeman who saw me close my street door at that unseemly hour knew that I was going to the great prize fight; the cabman who drove me to my destination was bursting with intelligence of the great prize fight; and the crowd who assembled round the railway station were either going with me to the great prize fight, or had come to see me go to the great prize fight . . . I obtained a seat in a rather overloaded double compartment of a second-class carriage. Behind me were a live lord, a live baronet, a member of Parliament, the very gentlemanly editor [Frank Dowling] of a distinguished sporting paper which has always done its utmost in the cause of fair-play, and honest dealing, an aristocratic Scotchman, a clergyman of the Church of England, and a renowned poet of the tender passions . . . There were dukes, lords, marquises, clergymen, actors, singers, managers, authors, reporters, painters and poets, mixed with plain country gentlemen, military officers, legislators, lawyers, barristers, merchants, card-sharpers, fathers of families who brought their sons, thieves, fighting-men, trainers, horse dealers, doctors, publicans, contractors, feather-weights, light-weights, middle-weights, heavy-weights, Americans of all classes, Irishmen of several classes, and Scotchmen also . . .

When the immortal Sayers stepped into the ring at about seven o'clock in the morning, he was received, like a popular performer, with a round of applause. His immortal face was a deep sallow brown, and looked like a square block of walnut wood. His expression was even a little more strongly marked for pugilism than that of most of his craft. He was slightly nervous upon facing the company.

His opponent, the immortal Heenan, next entered the ring, to be received with quite as much enthusiasm as the English Champion. He looked much fairer than Sayers in the face, and was equally nervous. His portraits had flattered him in the eyes of the British public. There are two styles of noses which all prize-fighters must be content to select from – one, presenting a flat, triangular appearance; the other, indented near the tip, and slightly turned up, so that you could hang a key upon it. The immortal Heenan had a moderate nose of the last pattern . . .

The two immortal heroes of the hour stood up, before each other in the most approved attitudes. Their left sides were advanced; their right arms were laid across their chests; their left arms were thrown out and drawn back, like the pawing leg of a horse. Their visitors watched every movement, for the present, in breathless silence; while their seconds peered at them from opposite corners, like wicket-keepers in a cricket-field. There was a forced laugh on each champion's face, that was meant to be agreeable. Their left feet kept tapping the ground, in a kind of dancing step; their heads were frequently thrown back, or bobbed down; and they skipped from side to side after aiming or parrying a blow. At last the first stage in the fight was reached, amidst uproarious applause; the immortal Sayers had succeeded in drawing 'first blood' from his antagonist . . .

An hour soon passed in this way, without any signs of the battle drawing to a conclusion. The immortal Sayer's face, with the sun full upon it, was like a battered copper tea-kettle; his right arm was stiff and helpless; and he was freely spitting blood. The immortal Heenan's right eye was closed up with a huge lump of blue flesh, produced by the Englishman's well-directed and determined blows; his upper lip, too, was puffed out, as if there were six rows of gums and teeth behind it. When Sayers gave a telling hit, he stopped and looked inquisitively at his adversary, to see what damage he had done; and after Heenan had knocked

George Newbold's photomontage of the scene at Farnborough in Hampshire, with Sayers and Heenan about to do battle in 1860. Many of the two hundred and fifty portraits were reassembled two years later for Newbold's picture of the contest between Jem Mace and Tom King.
REPRODUCED BY COURTESY OF T. TULLEY.

his opponent down, he turned to his seconds, threw up both his arms, and opened his swollen mouth in a gasping manner . . . When, at the end of two hours, and in the 37th round, the American got the neck of the Englishman across the rope, it was not the fault of the general multitude that murder was not presented to them as a crowning treat for their money. The American was requested to 'hold him' by a thousand voices on the ground, and in the trees; but at the height of the uproar the ring was broken, the referee was forced out of his place, and all became wild confusion.

Writing two months later, Dickens' erstwhile friend, William Makepeace Thackeray, while deploring prize-fighting on moral grounds, is full of praise for the courage and handihood shown by the combatants, and is particularly generous in his assessment of Tom Sayers as a representative of the indomitable national type:

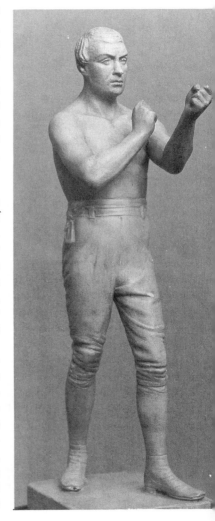

A lifelike statuette of Tom Sayers by the little-known sculptor Bezzi.
REPRODUCED BY COURTESY OF THE
NATIONAL PORTRAIT GALLERY, LONDON.

> I mean that fighting, of course, is wrong; but there are occasions when, &c. – I suppose I mean that one handed fight of Sayers is one of the most spirit-stirring little stories ever told: and with every love and respect for Morality – my spirit says to her, 'Do, for goodness sake, my dear madam, keep your true, and pure, and womanly, and gentle remarks for another day. Have the great kindness to stand a *leetle* aside, and just let us see one or two more rounds between the men. That little man with the one hand powerless on his breast facing yonder giant for hours, and felling him, too, every now and them!'

The enthusiastic writer went to some pains to deny that he was ever at ringside, but did admit to reading 'every word of the battle' the following morning. *The Times* had carried a 6,000-word fight report, and it is quite possible that the highly respectable creator of *Vanity Fair* could have gleaned enough information from this source to write what has since been mistaken for an eye-witness account. Whatever the truth, Thackeray was certainly the last famous author contemporary with the English prize-ring to leave us an impression of the intense national interest generated by a big fight.

Thackeray has also been widely credited with the authorship of some witty verses entitled 'The Fight of Sayerius and Heenanus', which appeared in an issue of the appropriately named periodical *Punch* subsequent to the great contest. Unfortunately for this theory the same lines have also been attributed, rather more convincingly, to one H. Cholmondeley Pennell, a regular contributor to the magazine. Subtitled 'A Lay of Ancient London', the excellent verses are a parody of Macaulay's popular 'Lays of Ancient Rome' and were supposed to have been recounted by an aged pug to his

The prolific illustrator Charles Keene shows William Makepeace Thackeray watching the Sayers versus Heenan fight, even though the writer denied being present. By the time that this wood-engraving was published in the 1879 edition of Thackeray's Roundabout Papers, *it was commonly believed that the writer* had *been at ringside, and he was no longer alive to deny it.*

great-grandchildren in 1920, far into the degenerate future. He begins:

> 'Tis but sixty years since
>   The times of which I speak,
> And yet the words I'm using
>   Will sound to you like Greek.
> What know ye, race of milksops,
>   Untaught of the P.R.,
> What stopping, lunging, countering,
>   Fibbing, or rallying are?
> What boots to use the *lingo*
>   When you have not the *Thing*?
> How paint to *you* the glories
>   Of BELCHER, CRIBB or SPRING, –
> To *you* whose sire turns up his eyes
>   At mention of the Ring?

Having recounted the fight in all its details the 'ancient gladiator' ends on a note of hope:

> And now my fists are feeble,
>   And my blood is thin and cold,
> But tis better than Old Tom to me
>   To recall those days of old.
> And may you, my great-grandchildren,
>   That gather round my knee,
> Ne'er see worse men, nor iller times
>   Than I and mine might be,
> Though England then had prize-fighters –
>   Even reprobates like me.

The handful of big fights which occurred on this side of the Atlantic following the great match of 1860 failed to attract the attention of the literati, or for that matter to arouse the interest of all but a few of the newly respectable general public. As the age of the prize-ring began to recede from memory, so it became imbued with the warm, rosy aura often assumed by distant and indistinct events. There now arose a new kind of pugilistic literature, based upon nostalgia and what ought to have happened, rather than upon the observation of what actually did.

Foremost among these pugilistic yarns came *Cashel Byron's Profession*, written in 1882 by George Bernard Shaw, at a time when, as he said himself, 'prize-fighting seemed to be dying out'. Painstakingly researched among the pages of *Boxiana*, by far the best part of the book is the preface, added upon publication in 1901, in which having evoked the good old days, Shaw brilliantly accounts for the popularity of fight scenes in English literature. He then proceeds to describe and explain the component parts of pugilistic genius, and states the reasons why this genius can eventually be, and indeed, usually is, beaten.

After the masterly preface it must be said that the story itself is something of a disappointment. Young Cashel, the genteel son of an actress, runs away from school and after various adventures fetches up in Australia, where he is befriended by the kindly ex-pug Skene. Under Skene's expert tutorage our hero soon discovers that he has the makings of a first-class boxer: he is in fact the pugilistic genius described in the preface. Having duly beaten all and sundry, the clean-limbed, well-mannered young prize-fighter and his mentor return to England, where, while in training to fight the contrastingly uncouth and insensitive William Paradise, he meets and eventually falls in love with an heiress. Having thrashed Paradise only to have the fight curtailed by police interference, Cashel retires from the profession, is reunited with his mother and discovers his absentee father to have been

The time-honoured method of dealing with foreigners and other undesirables is admirably demonstrated by the 'Bristol Bustler', at the expense of an escaped French prisoner of war, in one of Conan Doyle's series of chauvinistic short stories, The Exploits of Brigadier Gerard.

a lord. Our hero promptly inherits his father's estates, marries his heroine and they all live happily, etc. . .

In 1896, between the writing and eventual publication of *Cashel Byron*, there appeared that other splendid contribution to the nostalgic genre, *Rodney Stone* by Sir Arthur Conan Doyle. The plot and *dramatis personae* of this ripping yarn, set in the palmy days of the Regency, are remarkably similar to those already made familiar by Shaw, while Sir Arthur, a prize-fight enthusiast who kept boxing gloves in his pugilistically adorned bedroom, had also researched his subject thoroughly. The hero of the story is once more the estranged son of an aristocrat and an actress, but 'Boy Jim', as he is known, subsists by working at a blacksmith's forge with ex-prize-fighter 'Champion Harrison', and his toughness is perhaps a little more believable than that of Cashel Byron.

Rodney Stone contains some realistically portrayed fight scenes, as do the otherwise far-fetched but thoroughly readable series of short stories in which Conan Doyle draws upon his considerable knowledge of old-fashioned pugilism. *The Bully of Brocas Court*, featuring the mangled ghost of 'The Gasman', stands out as being particularly enjoyable, while an otherwise excellent tale, *The Croxley Master*, in which an athletic medical student beats a fearsome old pug at his own game and on his own ground, stretches belief beyond the bounds of acceptability. The author is as guilty as Bernard Shaw had been of gross classist misrepresentation.

Myths of this sort, written for public schoolboys, about public schoolboys and by public schoolboys, have served ever since as models for a host of similarly unlikely *Boys' Own* adventures: stories in which the hero is a well-educated and decent sprig of the nobility, or at least the gentry, who somehow, despite the disadvantages of an upbringing which does not include twelve or so hours of hard manual labour per day, spread over many years, coupled with an aggression born of hunger, still manages to thrash all manner of huge navvies and horny-handed coal-heavers. Later fictional heroes of the clean-punching type include such representatives of the middle and upper classes as boxing lawyers, boxing doctors and even boxing clergymen.

While not dismissing the advantages to be gained from clean living and the straight left, it would be most instructive to know how many generations of boys have been brought up on these stories and have placed implicit faith in them, only to be brutally and summarily disabused in real life.

SAYERS' & HEENAN'S GREAT FIGHT
FOR THE CHAMPIONSHIP.

Upon the seventeenth day of April,
  All in the morning soon,
The Yankee and the champion Sayers
  Prepared to meet their doom.
The train it ran along like wind,
  Coaches and cabs did fly,
Both men appeared determined
  To conquer or to die.

They fought like lions in the ring,
  Both men did boldly stand,
They two hours and six minutes fought,
  And neither beat his man.

Tom hit at the Benicia boy
  Right well you may suppose,
Heenan returned the compliment
  Upon the champion's nose.
Like two game cocks they stood the test,
  And each to win did try,
Erin-go-bragh, cried Heenan,
  I will conquer, lads, or die.

Cried Sayers, I will not give in,
  Nor to a Yankee yield,
The belt I mean to keep my boys,

Or die upon the field.
They together stood it manfully,
  Surprised all in the ring,
There was never such a battle, since
  Jack Langham tackled Spring.

Such fibbing and such up and down
  Lor, how the swells did shout,
Their ribs did nicely rattle,
  And their daylight near knocked out,
Tom Sayers let into Heenan,
  Heenan let into Tom,
While the Fancy bawled and shouted,
  Lads, my jolly lads, go on.

Two long hours and six minutes
  They fought, and the claret flew,
Sayers proved himself a brick, so did
  Yankee doodle doo.
The bets did fly about, my boys,
  And numbers looked with joy
On Sayers, the British champion,
  And the bold Benicia boy.

They both had pluck and courage,
  Each proved himself a man,

None better since the days of Spring
  In the British ring did stand.
Erin-go-bragh, cried Heenan,
  I want the English belt,
When Tom let fly, saying, I will die,
  Or keep the belt myself.

At length bounced in the peelers,
  And around the ring did jog,
So those heroes were surrounded
  By a lot of Hampshire hogs,
Who caused them to cut their stick,
  And from the fight refrain,
That they were both determined
  In the ring to meet again.

We admit Tom Sayers had his match
  One who did him annoy,
With lots of pluck and courage,
  Was the bold Benicia boy.
And when two heroes fight again,
  For honour and for wealth,
He that's the best man in the ring,
  Shall carry off the belt.

H. Disley, Printer, 57, High Street, St. Giles, London.

CHAPTER 4

POPULAR PRINTS AND VERSE

Three or four prints of dogs' heads; Grimaldi winning the Aylesbury steeple-chase; and Tom Crib, in a posture of defence, which did no credit to the science of that hero, if truly represented.

THOMAS HUGHES, *TOM BROWN'S SCHOOLDAYS, 1857*

A fairly typical cheap broadsheet of 1860, embellished with wood engravings. The verses would have been chanted by a pedlar or 'street-pitcher', to attract customers.

In his description of the decoration to be found on the walls of public schoolboys' studies during the early part of the last century, Thomas Hughes is remembering, from his own youth, the popularity among the fledgling squirearchy of sporting prints in general, and of cheap, crudely engraved portraits of boxers in particular.

The sporting print was, like pugilism, a peculiarly English art-form, and the period of time within which sporting prints enjoyed popularlity corresponds almost exactly with the time-limits of the prize-ring. First appearing late in the seventeenth century, sporting prints began to be fashionable during the latter part of the eighteenth century. They enjoyed a heyday in the Regency period before the genre died out in the middle of the reign of Queen Victoria.

There had been in existence, from the earliest days of English pugilism, 'fine art' engravings of prize-fights and fighters. This accomplished work of first-class artists was reproduced by the higly skilled and painstaking process of either mezzotint or aquatint engraving. The resulting products were, of course, beyond the means of both schoolboys and the poor illiterate majority of the population, who then, as now, possessed a voracious appetite for pictures and reports of sporting action.

Boxing held a predominant position among spectator sports of the time, and in lieu of today's tabloid press, there arose a huge demand for cheap mass-produced prints of the latest pugilistic heroes and events. Soon a large labour-intensive printing industry sprang up to cater for the unsophisticated tastes of the unread masses, who demanded narrative detail and strong colour, rather than skilful draughtsmanship or academic composition. The earliest of the resulting products were printed in black from either engraving or etching into copper plates, or from wood-engravings. The 'pulls' or prints could then be coloured by hand.

Etching was by far the most common technique employed, and was used extensively by such organisations as Messrs S. W. Fores of Piccadilly, a prolific publisher of sporting prints, who specialised in representations of the prize-ring. During the first quarter of the nineteenth century this one company must have produced literally tons of hand-coloured prints for the consumption of the sporting public. Fores' output ranges from striking depictions of Randall *v.* Martin and Cribb *v.* Molineaux to a host of anonymously produced full-length portraits representing every well-known bruiser of the time.

In execution these prints range from the skilful drawing and boisterous composition, complete with top-hatted seconds and bottle-holders, seen in the Randall and Martin epic of 1819, down through various stages of amusing amateurishness, to the unbelievably incompetent. The one thing which they all have in common is a delightfully robust immediacy, which seldom fails to please the modern viewer, any less than it appealed to his unsophisticated Regency forebears.

Fores' full-length portrait of Bill Eales has the following note inserted below the inscription: 'N.B. Portraits of all the Principal Pugilists will be executed in a uniform style.' Uniform they certainly were, but if a certain stilted similarity is discernible in much of what followed, it should be remembered that prize-fighting had been described by a contemporary writer as a religion, of which the fighters were the high priests. Cheap prints may therefore be seen as the icons of the cult, and must be expected to assume a ritualised and iconographic stiffness.

Ritual was also responsible for the conservatism evident in the costume worn by prize-fighters and seen in the prints. While seconds and bottle-holders are shown dressed in the latest fashion, whether of 1750 or 1850, the fighters themselves, right up until the end of the period of English pugilism in the late nineteenth century, always wear the breeches and stockings of the time of King George II and Jack Broughton, the only difference being the substitution of spiked boots for buckled shoes, necessitated by the change from fighting on a flat, unyielding wooden stage to the unpredictability of natural grass.

It will also be noticed that the majority of full-length portraits face to their left; this pose is favoured in order to facilitate the display of the faces of orthodox boxers (those that stand with the left hand and foot forward). In the few instances where they are shown facing the other way, they present their backs to the public, unless of course they are southpaws, who lead with the right, as in the case of Bendigo, Ned Turner or Bishop Sharpe.

The sporting pubs or 'lush cribs', with which London and the other prize-fighting centres abounded, were usually decorated with a selection of pugilistic etchings and engravings.

JACK RANDALL

born Nov. 25 1794. 5 feet 6 Inches high weighs 10, 6; has beaten Jack the Butcher in 20 minutes, Walton in 10 minutes, Geo. Dodd in 25 minutes, Ugly Berreck the Jew in 12 minutes, West Country Dick in 53. minutes, Holt in 25 minutes & only 8 rounds, Belasco in 56 minutes & only 7 rounds, Parish in 53 minutes & only 11 rounds, Turner in 2 Hours & 16 Minutes, Martin in 53 Minutes & many others of less note, in short he has never been beat.

Messrs S. W. Fores' hand-coloured etching depicts Jack Randall in 1820, at the pinnacle of his career.

Perhaps the most spectacular collection of pugilistic subject-matter was to be found at The Green Dragon in Soho, as we saw in Chapter 2, where the licensee, Joe Ward, kept his famous pugilistic picture gallery. Besides this 'Cabinet of the Fancy', as Ward's collection was known, his own parlour was packed with similar prize-fighting material, interspersed with patriotic subjects such as 'The Death of Nelson' and 'Duncan's Victory'.

At The Castle Tavern, High Holborn, in turn the licenced premises of ex-fighters Bob Gregson, Tom Belcher and Tom Spring, was to be found The Long Room which, between Gregson becoming publican in 1808 and Spring's death in

1851, became the virtual headquarters of prize-fighting. Egan describes it thus:

> The long-room is neatly fitted up, and lighted with gas, and the numerous sporting subjects, elegantly framed and glazed, have rather an imposing effect, upon the entrance of the visitor, among whom may be witnessed animated likenesses of the renowned JEM BELCHER and his daring competitor, that inordinate glutton, BURKE. The Champion, CRIB, and his tremendous opponent, MOLINEAUX. The father of the present race of boxers, Old JOE WARD. BOB GREGSON, in water-colours, by Mr EMERY, of Covent-Garden Theatre. TOM BELCHER, and his rival, the Jew phenomenon, DUTCH SAM. The scientfic contest between HUMPHREYS and MENDOZA. Portraits of GULLEY, the *Game* CHICKEN, &c. With a variety of other subjects, including one of the dog, 'TRUSTY,' the champion of the canine race, in fifty battles, and the favourite animal of the late *Jem Belcher,* the gift of Lord Camelford.

The Castle Tavern also provided the venue for 'convivial meetings' at which singing, or 'chaunting' as it was called, played a major part in the celebration of a pugilistic victory or the latest match-making. At these largely alcoholic occasions, the chair was often taken by Egan himself, who also took the opportunity of preserving many of these 'Chaunts for the Fancy' in the pages of *Boxiana*.

Egan introduces the genre in his magnum opus with his own ditty 'The Lads of the Fancy' – which was sung to the tune of 'The Land of Sweet Erin':

> You Lads of the Fancy, who wish to impart
> The tokens of friendship and soundness of heart,
> To Belcher's repair, at the Castle so strong,
> Where he'll serve you all well, and you'll hear a good song.
> The company cheerful, and sporting's the go –
> Though milling's the theme, you'll not meet with a foe;
> But each in good humour, enjoying his pipe,
> With tales of the Fancy – and knowledge of life!
> Then let us be merry,
> While drinking our sherry,
> For friendship and harmony can't last too long
> Be still our endeavour,
> That nothing will sever
> The Lads of the Fancy at the Castle so strong!

Ballads of this sort were sometimes printed in the form of broadsheets, or appended to portraits of fighters. Set to popular tunes, they were meant to be sung in taverns and beerhouses, and usually contained a chorus in which the assembled company was expected to join.

As with mass-produced pictorial representations of pugilistic contests, great impetus for chaunting was provided by the bitter rivalry between Dan Mendoza and Richard Humphries which culminated in their three 'public contests for superiority' of 1788, '89 and '90. The second fight in the series took place at Stilton, and was won by Mendoza when Humphries fell to avoid punishment. In his autobiography, Mendoza, with no trace of false modesty, quotes the following song, which he tells us was one of several: 'made on the subject of the late victory [and] sung with great applause at several convivial meetings'.

A cheap wood-engraving published in London in about 1790, as part of a reading primer. The spelling of 'Humphfries' leaves a little to be desired.

O my Dicky, my Dicky, and O Dicky my dear,
Such a wonderful Dicky is not to be found far nor near;
For Dicky was up, up, up and Dicky was down, down,
    down,
And Dicky was backwards and forwards, and Dicky was
    round, round, round.

My Dicky was all the delight of half the genteels in town;
Their tables were scarcely compleat, unless my Dicky sat
    down;
So very polite, so genteel, such a soft complaisant face,
What a damnable shame to be spoil'd by a curst little
    Jew from Duke's Place.

Chorus:
For Dicky, he stopt with his head,
Was hit through his guard ev'ry round, Sir,
Was fonder of falling than fighting,
And therefore gave out on the ground, Sir.

Mendoza's jeering tone may perhaps be forgiven when we remember an incident which occurred during the first fight between these bitter rivals in the previous year. This incident is depicted in one of the earliest narrative prints associated with prize-fighting, and *Boxiana* relates the circumstances from a contemporary report:

Mendoza, who in the early part of the fight had drove Humphries upon the rail of the stage, and while the latter was upon the balance, aimed a blow at his ribs which must have finished the battle, but Johnson caught it. The umpires considered it a knock-down blow, and that Johnson was correct.

The Gillray print, entitled 'Foul Play', shows Humphries' second, Tom Johnson, the current champion, perpetrating this blatantly unfair action. Poor Mendoza, after fighting on

with varied success for another half-hour, fell on the rain-soaked stage, badly sprained his ankle, 'and was reluctantly compelled to acknowledge the superiority of the Christian'.

It was after this fight that Humphries wrote to his absent patron the laconic note: 'Sir, I have done the Jew, and am in good health.' That Mendoza won the second and third of his fights with Humprhies did nothing to endear him to 'impartial' John Bull, who continued to evince considerable prejudice towards 'the Jew', as Mendoza, the first of his race to gain prominence as a boxer, was always known. One reading primer, published in London at the time, even goes so far as to represent Mendoza as the despised racial stereotype, complete with straggly beard, looking far more like Shylock, or a model for Fagin, than a puglist.

The three fights between Mendoza and Humphries produced more prints, chaunts and memorabilia than any other sporting event of the eighteenth century. There is even an extensive series of delightful, transfer-printed Staffordshire beer jugs showing the combatants setting-to, shadowed by their seconds and bottle-holders.

The astute Mendoza, who well understood the value of publicity, was quick to cash in on the fame gained by his contests with Humphries. He travelled the United Kingdom and Ireland demonstrating his methods of defence and attack and teaching any young gentlemen who could spare a fee the rudiments of the noble art.

A playbill produced at Stafford while Mendoza was demonstrating his art during the intervals of a play at the town's theatre contained the following assurance:

'Foul Play, or Humphries and Johnson a Match for Mendoza', shows Tom Johnson interposing his considerable bulk to save his man from injury. Gillray mockingly dedicated this engraving to Wilson Braddyl Esq., the chief backer of Humphries.
REPRODUCED BY COURTESY OF JOHN MURRAY LTD.

The ladies are respectfully informed that there is neither violence nor indecency that can offend the most delicate of their sex: as an affirmation of which Mr Mendoza has by repeated desire, performed before Their Majesties and the Royal Family.

Jack Broughton and James Figg had earlier produced both handbills and advertisements for their London-based booths, but that was in the days before pugilism became illegal, and even then neither had the nerve to actually claim royal patronage in print.

Back once more in London, Mendoza was debarred from taking money for demonstrating what was strictly an illegal activity, so he hit upon the novel idea of selling engraved portraits of himself for half a crown, and granting 'free' admission to his sparring rooms upon the engraving being presented at the door.

Mezzotint engraving of Mendoza from the full-length painting by Jean Robineau.

Daniel Mendoza the Pugilist
from the Original Painting by Robineau
in the Possession of
T. Hotchkin Esq.r
Published Jan.y 1st 1789, by John Fagg, Dorset Street, London.

After the Mendoza *v*. Humphries fights, no event or series of events claimed anything like so much publicity, or produced as many memorabilia for another twenty years, although in the intervening years there appeared good, bad and indifferent representations of The Game Chicken, Jem Belcher, John Gully and their contemporaries.

The next fight to arouse such huge public interest was the second match between the Champion, Tom Cribb and American Negro, Tom Molineaux, which took place at Thistleton Gap, Leicestershire in 1811. Cribb had already beaten this opponent in the previous year, but only with the help of his second, Joe Ward of Green Dragon fame, who, by falsely accusing Molineaux of secreting hard substances in his fists, gained extra time for Cribb to recover consciousness after a particularly severe round. The public demanded a more resounding victory than this, and accordingly the men met for a second time.

Ward was again the champion's attendant, but his time-gaining services were not required on this occasion. When Cribb, trained by the famous pedestrian Captain Barclay, reduced from over 16 stones to a fiit, hard 13½ stone, this time put his superiority beyond doubt, his countrymen went wild with joy.

This fight, the most famous from pugilism's 'golden age', launched a profusion of cheap engraved portraits and full-length figures, in addition to the more sophisticated productions of Rowlandson, Cruikshank and Géricault.

There also appeared more Staffordshire beer jugs and mugs, transfer-printed with scenes from what was regarded as a great national victory. In addition, several pairs of charming figurines of the protagonists were produced, stripped for action just as they were in front of twenty thousand spectators, many of whom had travelled the ninety-odd miles from the metropolis to be present.

This event, which removed the threat of foreign competition for nearly four decades, also provided the theme for a veritable rash of nationalist chaunts, of which the following is a fairly typical example:

A New Song Called The Mill

Tune – 'The Arethusa'

Come all you jolly millers bold,
Whose hearts are cast of British mould,
A story I will now unfold
   Of the gallant fighting Black man.
He's come to mill our champion Cribb,
And doth declare he will him fib,
No fear that he will ever jib
   On the Eighteenth of December.

His friends, all Yankees, they did meet,
To stump the brads for the look'd for feat,
   And support their country hero;
And as the bets they now do go,
Poor Cribb, it seems, must be laid low.
For the Black will strike a serious blow
   On the Eighteenth of December.

Now Cribb, a man of a black trade,
Of black or white was ne'er afraid
And hitherto hath prov'd a blade
   Worthy of high renown, Sir;
But his friends, we hear, look very glum,
And no few swells are nearly dumb,
For fear he should dislike the fun
   On the Eighteenth of December.

But like a Briton, for its cause,
At such a challenge could not pause,
And said he'd shew him English laws,
   As none but we can boast of.
But should our champion now be beat,
Contending of this gallant feat,
To our milling lads and swells so great
   And the Eighteenth of December.

Not great poetry, perhaps, but not so bad either when compared to the poetical effusions of Cribb's earlier opponent, Bob Gregson. Having retired from active participation in the events of the ring to the comparative peace and quiet of the licensed victualling profession, Gregson, with encouragement from Egan, now styled himself 'Poet Laureate to the heroic race of pugilists'.

The final verse of an appalling chaunt composed by 'Bob of Wigan, time-honoured Lancashire', in commemoration of Cribb's great victory, is entitled 'British Lads and Black Millers' and comprehensively demonstrates not only the author's poetic ineptitude but the violent chauvanist feeling current at the time:

The garden of freedom is the British land we live in,
And welcomes every slave from his banish'd isle,
Allows them to impose on a nation good and generous,
To incumber and pollute our native soil.
But John Bull cried out aloud,
We're neither poor nor proud,
But open to all nations, let them come from where they will.
The British lads that's here,
Quite strangers are to fear,
Here's TOM CRIBB, with bumpers round, for he can them mill!

Even the biased Egan, a regular at Gregson's pub, had to admit that Bob 'did not possess the terseness and originality of Dryden or the musical cadence and correctness of Pope'.

Undoubtedly the most important item produced in celebration of Cribb's triumph, was the first volume of Egan's *Boxiana* itself, published in 1812. In addition to a full-length portrait of Cribb and a pull-out representation of the fight, *Boxiana* contains copies of well-known engravings of bygone contests, such as those between Tom Johnson and Isaac Perrins and of the third in the series between Mendoza and Humphries. There is also a somewhat mixed collection of bruisers' faces, past and present, which exhibits varying degrees of artistic competence.

George Sharples was employed to illustrate volumes two and three, a task which he accomplished with consumate skill,

Bob Gregson's impressive physique was much in demand for modelling at the Royal Academy. This side-line provided the impecunious boxer with some much needed cash, for Bob was remarkably unsuccessful as a fighter, a publican and as 'Poet Laureate to the heroic race of pugilists'.

producing a dozen remarkably well observed and lifelike, if somewhat idealised, head and shoulders portraits of the leading pugilists of the time. When in 1824 the idiosyncratic Egan quarrelled with his publisher, and the even more eccentric 'Jon Bee' was taken on as editor of volume four, either the new editor or the publisher saw fit to replace Sharples' competent work with eight full-length figures, drawn by one Read. Charming though these stiffly posed figures are, the difference in skill between Read and Sharples is enormous and is underlined by the fact that the same engraver was employed to translate the drawings onto copper plates. Despite the very apparent falling off of quality, Bee had the cheek to insert the following 'puff' at the foot of his foreword: 'Regarding the introduction of full-length Portraits instead of Busts, they further expect the Purchasers' approbation; for the alteration in this respect was only effected at considerable expense.'

When for the final two volumes Egan found a new publisher, the quality of illustrations immediately improved and the portraits revert to the head and shoulders type, produced by such consumate draughtsmen as Thomas Wageman.

With regard to chaunts, if at any time Egan was unable to find sufficient to fill his pages, he was not above providing the deficiency himself, as can be seen from the verses he wrote in praise of Jack Carter, Tom Oliver, Scroggins, Jack Randall, Ned Turner, Tom Spring and every other pugilist of note.

One of his better endeavours was written towards the end of 1814. Entitled 'Dutch Sam; or the tears of Dukes Place', it tells the sad but all too familiar story of a hitherto invincible boxer having one fight too many. 'Dutch Sam' was the ring-name of an East End Israelite named Samuel Elias or Elias Samuel, who succeeded Mendoza as champion of Jewry. Sam boasted that he trained on gin, the consequences of which are related in the final verse:

> Then a pigeon from Moulsey was sent to Duke's Place,
> With a label that signified all SAM's disgrace;
> That the tribes might hedge off, as for old clothes they
>   range,
> 'Mid the beaux of the west, or the flats near the Change;
> While Israel's brown children in sympathy roar,
> 'Have you heard of Dutch Sam?' – No! 'My Cot, he's
>   done o'er.'

However, the following is a fair example of what Egan usually passed off as lyrics:

> You admirers of Boxing attend to my lay,
> And I'll chaunt you the feats of a prime day's play,
> At fam'd Moulsey Hurst on July twenty-third,
> Of the three bravest battles that ever occurr'd!
>
> Chaunt away, chaunt, chaunt, chaunt away.

Not to be outdone, Bob Gregson composed verses in honour of the fight between Randall and Turner at Crawley Down in 1818, the best part of which is a chorus which runs:

> With a filaloo trillalo,
> Whack, fal lal de dal di de do.

In mitigation it should be remembered that this chorus would sound much less absurd when sung, and that popular lyrics have seldom translated well into cold print.

A few contests were commemorated with medals, the earliest being that in which Tom Johnson skilfully cut down the huge challenger Isaac Perrins in 1789. Just one year later, the head of astute Dan Mendoza appeared on a half-penny token, which bore a reverse design of boxers in attitude and the words 'Fashionable Amusement'. Never one to let up on a money making venture, Mendoza again appeared in 1791 facing his future opponent Bill Warr on a token which seems to have been struck as a pre-fight announcement. The fight on Hungerford Downs in 1821 between Bill Neat of Bristol and London-based Midlander, Tom Hickman 'The Gasman', was also celebrated numismatically, as Jon Bee informs us in volume four of *Boxiana*:

A pair of bronze medals produced at Birmingham to commemorate the contest between champion Tom Johnson and his giant challenger Isaac Perrins. The fight took place near Banbury in 1789 and was cleverly won by Johnson, who retained his title in one hour and a quarter. The reverse design of both medals incorporates a quotation from Virgil's Aeneid, 'BELLA, HORRIDA BELLA' (Wars, horrid wars).

> A medal of excellent workmanship was produced at Birmingham, worthy of being preserved by all true lovers of British sports, that will do honour to the collection of any *virtuoso*, and remind the aspirant after fistic honours to what imperishable materials he is dedicating his labours and his fame.

The obverse shows the two pugilists squaring up to each other, while the reverse legend reads 'Blood, Bone, Action and Game, The Sportsman's Delight'. Blood, Bone, Action and Game all formed prominent features of this brutal fight, which was immortalised by Hazlitt who travelled down over night from London to be present at what was expected by many to be a mere formality for Hickman, but which, in the event, turned out quite differently:

> When Gas-light shares fell cent per cent
> And thus the battle ended.
> The Cockney's tune was altered soon,
> In purse and spirits undone,
> As on the rack they toddled back
> With empty clies to London.
>
> Come Bristol boys, let's claim the bays
> Come Daffies, spruce and clever,
> With loud huzzas proclaim his praise
> Sing Champion Neat for ever.

In fact the Bristol boys sang Champion Neat for a mere sixteen months, at the end of which time their hero was beaten to a standstill by Tom Spring and suffered a broken arm into the bargain.

The two great fights between Spring and the Irish Champion Jack Langan which took place in the mid 1820s, and marked the end of the great days of pugilism, produced very little in the way of engravings. There are however, some single

colour pottery plaques, produced yet again in Staffordshire, on which the figures are shown in the usual stereotyped attitude, against backgrounds which have rather more in common with the Chinese cups and saucers popular at the time than with either Worcester Racecourse or the wooden stage at Chichester where the fights actually took place.

The wooden stage at Warwick upon which in 1824 Tom Cannon beat Josh Hudson for the championship vacated by Spring, bears a strong resemblance in a contemporary wood-engraving, to that at Tyburn which played such a prominent part in the 'Last Dying Confessions' so popular at that time of public executions.

There is a marked similarity to his more usual gallows literature in the sombre verses printed by the indefatigable Jemmy Catnatch of Seven Dials, following the fatal championship fight between Deaf Burke and Simon Byrne in 1833:

Mourn, Erin's sons, your hero brave; his loss all may
  deplore,
Brave Simon Byrne, that hero bold, alas! he is no more;
For courage true and science good he never was afraid,
Of Larkins, Sampson, Ward, McKay, could ne'er be
  dismayed.

The first fight between Spring and Langan took place on Worcester racecourse, where the scene at ringside was rather less orderly than that implied by the sedate gathering shown on this rare black and white Staffordshire plaque.

SPRING AND LANGAN

Chorus.
Mourn! Erin mourn, your loss deplore; poor Simon's
dead and gone.
An hero brave laid in the grave as ever the sun shone on.

On Thursday, May the 30th day, brave Simon took the
ring,
Back'd by Jem Ward the champion, likewise by gallant
Spring,
To fight Burke for two hundred pounds, a man of
courage bold,
To stop reports that with Ward the battle he had sold.

Both men stript, then shook hands, when began a great
display,
For thirty rounds shouts did resound, brave Byrne will
win the day,
But Burke, as hard as beaten steel, and deaf to all their
cries,
When all thought he was beaten dead, time call'd, he up
did rise.

*This crude wood-engraving,
representing the fight between
Tom Cannon and Josh Hudson on
Warwick racecourse in 1824, strongly
resembles the popular public hanging
scenes of the time. The grossly
overweight Hudson, who was knocked
out in twenty minutes, might easily be
regarded as the condemned man.*
REPRODUCED BY COURTESY OF
MARY EVANS PICTURE LIBRARY.

It's knock down for knock down they fought till the
    ninety-ninth round,
When Burke gave a tremendous blow, which fell'd him
    to the ground,
And time being call'd, Simon's backers found it was in
    vain,
Brave Byrne he fell his last that time, he could not rise
    again.

To St Alban's he was convey'd, assistance came with
    speed.
The sufferings that he did undergo would make a heart
    to bleed,
He sigh'd and said – 'It's not the blow distresses me so
    sore,
I did my best, I've lost!' he sigh'd; brave Byrne was then
    no more.

Few hours before brave Simon died, these words he was
    heard to say,
'Three years ago, this very day, I fought Sandy McKay,
I caused his death, I meet the same, farewell my infants
    all,
Dear wife, farewell, in heaven again to meet I hope we
    shall.'

The solemn bell, its awful knell did call our hero brave,
Hundreds did cry as he pass'd by unto the silent grave,
And now the green sod covers o'er that once manly
    frame,
Say, was there e'er his like before, or will there be again?

When Burke and seconds of brave Bryne did hear that he
    was dead,
To France and other parts for safety off they quickly fled,
And may the contributions which these valiant men have
    made,
Be followed up with spirit for his wife and children's aid.

In passing, it is heartening to relate that an appeal was made for the widow, by Vincent Dowling, the editor of *Bell's Life*, headed by himself with five guineas. Within a week Burke, his seconds and the seconds of Byrne each added a similar amount, and in a short time the considerable sum of £262 was raised for the unfortunate woman.

Both prints and ballads become less frequent from this period as interest in the prize-ring declined during the early years of the Victorian era. Charles Hunt's well-known full-length aquatints of 'Deaf' Burke and 'Bendigo', produced in the years around 1840, together with the same engraver's representation of 'The Great Fight between Broome and Hannan for £1000', may be seen as a final manifestation of the old pre-railway, pre-photographic Hanoverian world. Although we will have to wait for almost another twenty years before photography makes an appearance upon the boxing scene, the age of the photograph is foreshadowed by the representation in this splendid aquatint of so many well-known spectators, in addition to the combatants and their, alas no longer top-hatted, attendants.

Huddled at ringside on a cold January morning in 1841 may be seen the ex-champions Tom Cribb, Tom Spring, Peter Crawley and 'Deaf' Burke, rubbing shoulders with rising stars Johnny Walker, 'Hammer' Lane and a handful of staunch 'Gentlemen amateurs'. While attentively sitting with notebooks just outside the ropes are Vincent Dowling and Renton Nicholson, representatives of the leading sporting newspapers, *Bell's Life* and *Town*.

Ballads and chaunts continued to be published in the form of broadsheets, one of which, produced following particularly disgraceful scenes at a championship fight, ending with fouls and a full-scale riot, informs us in a rollicking style, which suggests that nothing untoward took place, that:

JOHNNY WALKER

This full-colour lithograph is one of a series representing the top fighters of the 1840s. Each of the portraits is remarkable for its charmingly incompetent draughtsmanship.

> On the ninth day of September,
> Eighteen hundred and forty five,
> From London down to Nottingham
> The roads were all alive;
> Oh! such a sight was never seen
> Believe me it was so,
> Tens of thousands went to see the fight,
> With Ben Caunt and Bendigo.
>
> With their hit away and slash away,
> So manfully you see,
> Ben Caunt has lost and Bendigo
> Has gained the victory.

Although from this period prize-fighting became distinctly out of fashion, and by mid-century the art of the sporting engraver had largely joined it, there were still published several splendidly naïve portraits of Bendigo, Ben Caunt and their lesser contemporaries in the mid-forties. But we are hard pushed to find any pictorial representations or ballads commemorating the 'Tipton Slasher' and other leading fighters of the 1850s.

An unexpected revival in pugilism occurred in the late fifties with the emergence of Tom Sayers as champion, a renewed interest which was accompanied by exploitation of the lithographic printing technique. Lithography had been around since the early eighteen hundreds but had only really become popular in mid-century with the substitution of light-weight zinc plates for the cumbersome limestones from which the process takes its name.

A lithographic image is produced by drawing *onto* a smooth flat surface with greasy ink or a crayon, as opposed to engraving *into* a copper plate or wood block. This process at its most basic level requires very little skill, while on the other hand copper and wood engraving had required considerable practice with a sharp edged implement to produce even the most rudimentary line image. Whereas the necessarily skilful engraver into copper might sometimes enhance an original drawing of questionable technique, the lithographic 'draughts-man' could be, and all too often was, almost devoid of any artistic ability.

However, among the host of lithographic prize-ring prints which appear at about this time are some which, with their quaint draughtsmanship and less than perfect knowledge of human anatomy, exude a charm equal to, but quite distinct from, that of the earlier copper or wood engravings.

At the same time the advent and spread of photography allowed its early practitioners to do a brisk trade in accurate portraits of the current heroes. Unfortunately, sitting bolt upright and perfectly still in a photographer's chair during the long exposure then necessary to obtain an image is not the best way in which to capture the character of a sitter. In the case of the rather glum portraits of Tom Sayers which have survived, the author of *Pugilistica* informs us: 'The photographs which figure in the print-shop windows do not convey

Coloured aquatint by Charles Hunt after Henry Heath, depicting most of the leading fighters and their patrons gathered at ringside in 1841 to witness Johnny Broome of Birmingham cause a major upset by beating the experienced Londoner Jack Hannan, for a stake of £1,000.

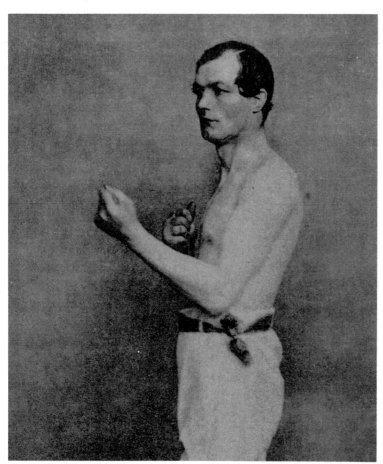

Nat Langham poses for his portrait, in a photograph taken at some time following the skilful middleweight's defeat of the otherwise invincible Tom Sayers in 1853.

a fair idea of Tom's good-tempered and often merry expression: he seems to have been taken when filled with the contemplation of the seriousness of having one's "counterfeit presentment" multiplied and sent forth to the world.'

Photography also enabled 'mug shots' to be taken immediately after an important fight, for sale to a public appreciative of contusions, cauliflower ears, bunged-up eyes and split lips. These homely and distinguishing marks of the sitters' profession were sometimes engraved onto wood blocks for reproduction in publications not yet capable of printing dot halftones, but although an engraver might enhance injuries and thereby encourage sales, the process of turning the immediacy of a photographic image into a 'drawn' engraving can only weaken the present-day viewer's belief in the facial damage so engagingly displayed.

Lithographic printers seem to have been amongst the earliest to realise the potential of mechanically transferring a photographic image onto a printing plate, a process used to great effect to portray the spectators as well as the combatants at some of the big fights of the latter bare-knuckle era.

This use of photography constitutes a last flourish of the art

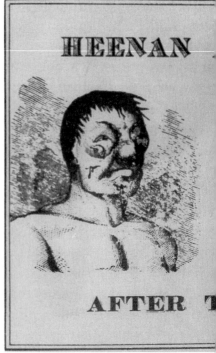

of the sporting print and coincides with the final championship contests of Tom Sayers. The edition of *Bell's Life* published one week after the great fight of 1860 contains this announcement:

> Mr Newbold's Great Picture of The Fight is nearing completion . . . as every likeness is being engraved from a photograph by Watkins, it will be such a memento of the event as will prove invaluable to all sportsmen . . . Many of the Corinthian patrons of the science will be included, but of course they do not desire their names to appear in print.

As camera shutter speeds could not yet cope with moving crowd scenes, the portraits, all 250 of them, were taken individually in the photographer's studio. The resulting photographs ('which may also be had singly') were then painstakingly montaged around a drawn boxing-ring and published as an exact representation of the scene in a Hampshire meadow when, at precisely 7.29 a.m. on 17 April 1860, the by now immortal Sayers and Heenan set to.

This event both shocked and thrilled hypocritical Victorian society, and for the last time in the history of the English prize-ring produced an enormous number of prints and associated memorabilia. There were, besides Newbold's 'Great Picture', several other large representations based on photographic reference, including one by ex-champion-turned-artist Jem Ward, which was sold together with a numbered key to the spectators' portraits, or at least those spectators who could be relied upon not to sue for defamation of character.

In addition, there were crude woodcuts with verses bad enough to recall the poetic efforts of Bob Gregson, silk scarves, song sheets, and a charming and very popular Staffordshire pottery group, showing the combatants locked in combat, each with a left fist glued forever to the face of his antagonist.

Both Sayers and Heenan are shown standing in the crowd, when the enterprising George Newbold repeated his huge photographic operation to commemorate the occasion on which the badly beaten Tom King landed a wild punch, which deprived Jem Mace of the championship at Thames Haven in 1862. No doubt this event afforded the entrepreneur an opportunity to re-use some of the studio portraits of the regular fancy, taken two years earlier.

These latter-day Corinthians who are to be seen gathered at ringside with their picnic hampers, cigars and magnums of champagne, had travelled down to the north Kent marshes by the new railway train or paddle-steamer.

The prize-ring, sporting prints and Fancy Chaunts, along with stage-coaches and sailing ships, were already becoming little more than a blurred memory.

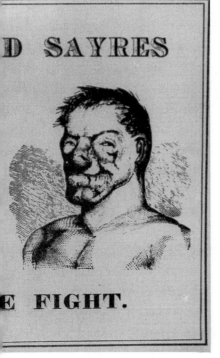

Spectacular facial damage and bad spelling, both add to the charm of this wood-engraving, published in 1860.

CHAPTER 5

TROPHIES AND BELTS

Then Achilles brought out prizes for the violent boxing match; for the winner he led forth and tethered a sturdy mule; and for the loser set down a two-handled cup.

HOMER, *THE ILLIAD*, BOOK 23

On this trophy, dating from the time of Alexander the Great in the fourth century BC, a pair of muscular boxers exchange blows, while a third looks on and adjusts his cestus.
REPRODUCED BY COURTESY OF
THE TRUSTEES OF THE BRITISH MUSEUM.

So begins the earliest extant description of a prize-fight, proof that the practice of awarding trophies to boxers dates back at least to the eighth century BC. On this occasion the cup was regarded as a consolation prize, while the winner obtained a far more useful beast of burden.

Seven hundred years later, after the boxing match between Entellus and Dares described by the Roman poet Virgil, the victorious Entellus received a steer, the brains of which he proceeded to knock out with his leather bound fist, as proof of his forbearance to the unconscious but still breathing Dares, who had to be content with a sword and helmet.

In addition to the laurel wreaths awarded to victors in the ancient Olympic games, successful boxers in the days of Greece and Rome were sometimes presented with beautifully decorated amphorae containing valuable oil or wine, a custom which would seem to be the direct ancestor of the modern practice of awarding cups to winners. The Emporer Caligula is reputed to have gone one better when, in the first century AD, he rewarded his victorious African boxers with young and noble virgins.

However, money and fame seem to have been the sole prizes contended for by the pugilists of eighteen-century England, and we know that Jack Broughton died possessed of both fame and a considerable fortune. Tom Johnson, on the other hand, was forced out of retirement by his propensity for dice and he is reported to have lost his tremendous ring earnings of £5,000 as well as a hard-won reputation by his addiction to 'shaking the elbow'. Gambling in all forms seems to have been the downfall of many early fighting men, and Dan Mendoza, describing an incident which occurred whilst on tour in Scotland with Tom Fewtrell, tells us that:

Pugilistic men, when they have derived money from their exertions, seldom refrain from venturing it at cards, dice, or some kind of gambling; and Fewtrell was not unlike his brethren in this respect; for having gained some money by our tour, he was never easy but when he was playing.

It was whilst exhibiting in the Scottish capital that Mendoza was presented with a gold medal by the Edinburgh Gymnastic Society as a 'testimonial of the high opinion they unanimously held of me'. This presentation took place in 1790 or '91 and appears to be the earliest instance of a British boxer being presented with a lasting trophy in addition to hard cash. As in many matters, the polished Mendoza was some years ahead of his contemporaries, most of whom continued to gamble and drink themselves into obscurity and oblivion with no more lasting evidence of their exertions than broken noses and cauliflower ears.

By the beginning of the nineteenth century various rich patrons of the sport were keen to reward leading bruisers with more tangible tokens of their esteem, and Tom Cribb would seem to be the first boxer to be awarded a trophy in recognition of the English championship. The resulting presentation and the events leading up to it are described by Pierce Egan:

> ... a splendid dinner was given at Gregson's chop-house, by a large party of pugilistic amateurs ... the company did not depart till they unanimously voted the Champion – A SILVER CUP, valued at Fifty Guineas, as a memorial of the

Far from being the 'penny plain, tuppence coloured' class of print available to the proletariat, this powerful portrait of Mendoza, engraved by James Gillray in 1790, sold for three shillings, the equivalent of two days' agricultural wages.

One of a series of popular early nineteenth century Staffordshire jugs. The figures of Cribb and Molineaux oppose each other on this side, while on the other is a poem in praise of British boxing.

Gillray ad viv. del. et fec.   MENDOZA.   Pub.^d April 14 by J. Lewis & sold by J. Aitkin, Castle St.

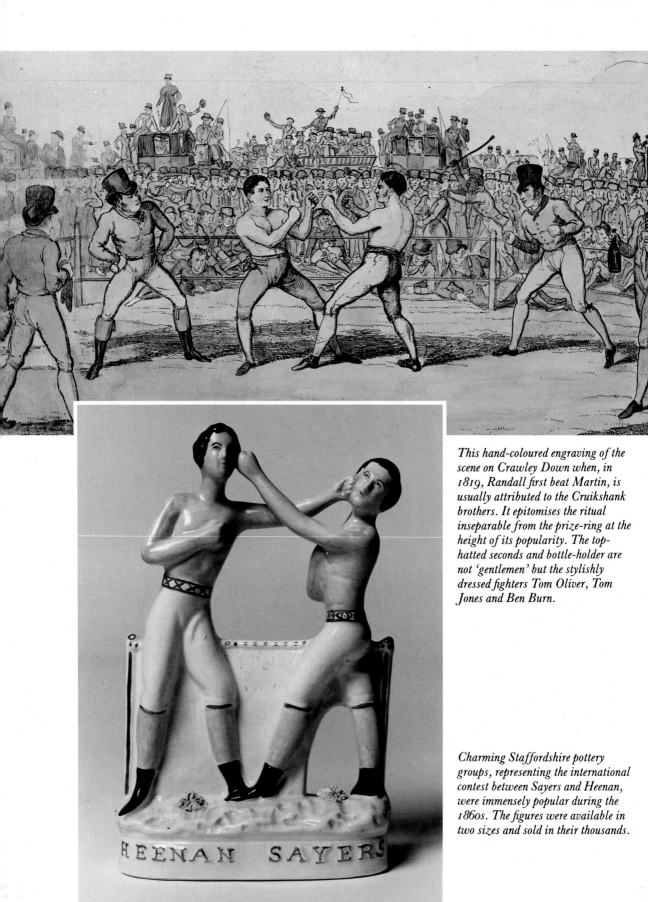

This hand-coloured engraving of the scene on Crawley Down when, in 1819, Randall first beat Martin, is usually attributed to the Cruikshank brothers. It epitomises the ritual inseparable from the prize-ring at the height of its popularity. The top-hatted seconds and bottle-holder are not 'gentlemen' but the stylishly dressed fighters Tom Oliver, Tom Jones and Ben Burn.

Charming Staffordshire pottery groups, representing the international contest between Sayers and Heenan, were immensely popular during the 1860s. The figures were available in two sizes and sold in their thousands.

HEENAN SAYERS

high opinion which the Sporting World ... held of his uniform courage, and superiority in his pugilistic combats – induced to enter the ring, (after having positively declined pugilism in general) on the score of nationality ... to prevent a FOREIGNER [Cribb had recently defeated the American negro Molineaux for the second time] from triumphing over the heroes of England. The subscriptions for the above purpose proving so ample, the sum was increased, and a silver cup of eighty guineas value was presented to the Champion at the Castle Tavern, Holborn, on ... the 2nd of December, 1811, at a dinner appointed for that purpose.

These presentation dinners which involved eating and more especially drinking to a degree hardly credible to all but the most determined of modern trenchermen and topers, were to become a popular fixture in the pugilistic calendar over the next twenty years:

> ... after the cloth was removed and the usual toasts of loyalty had been given, Mr Emery [Robert Emery, the well-known comedian] ... was called upon to fulfil the wishes of the present company, when the Cup was immediately produced, the Son of Thespis rose, and gave 'Cribb – the Champion of England.'

Mr Emery then delivered a speech in praise of the retiring hero, which concluded with the following well-chosen words:

> However intoxicated the cup or its contents may at any future period make you, I am sufficiently persuaded the gentlemen present, and the sons of John Bull in general, will never consider you have a cup too much.

The cup was then filled with wine, passed round and swiftly emptied, while the reticent champion stammered out his thanks. '*Chaunting* then became "the order of the day", and among the toasts and songs given upon this occasion considerable originality appeared.'

At this point Egan takes the opportunity to introduce six close-set pages of 'the most admired Chaunts, sung at the convivial meetings of the Fancy'.

Meanwhile:

> Harmony reigned, and the Champion expressed his gratitude to his leading patrons, Sir Henry Smyth, Bart., Captain Barclay, Shirwell Harrison, Esq... and, drank their health with marked animation and respect; the Cup being put round, upon its arrival into the hands of Mr Jackson, Gulley, Gregson, and the veteran Joe Ward,

. . . the company, as a mark of esteem for their past services, loudly cheered those celebrated heroes of the fist.

No doubt the cheering, chaunting and passing round of the cup continued well into the small hours.

The cup itself was a rather handsome drinking vessel, supported by a classical pugilist, kneeling in the pose of Atlas holding the globe, while on the lid was a representation of Britannia brandishing the Union Jack and blowing her own trumpet. Engraved with a bogus coat of arms and one of Egan's favourite Shakespearian quotations, the *tout ensemble* stood about fifteen inches high, weighed nearly 5 lbs and was completed by a pair of ornate baroque handles.

Although the dinner officially marked Cribb's retirement from the ring, he could not be persuaded to resign the championship until 1822, in which year the old warrior finally

The engraving of Tom Cribb's cup from Boxiana *was accompanied by Egan's description of the sham coat of arms.*

acknowledged the advancing years and handed over the title to his protegé, Tom Spring. The occasion was marked by the presentation to the retiring champion of another trophy. This took the form of a lion-skin belt, the dimensions of which eloquently attest to the additional rotundity of form gained during his easy years behind the bar of The Union Arms in Panton Street. Amid vociferous cheering the belt was fastened around Cribb's ample waist by means of a silver clasp in the form of a pair of lion's paws, further decoration being provided by a pair of silver plaques engraved with a list of the many hard-fought contests which comprised his long and illustrious career.

In the same year the *Fancy Gazette* recorded that the services of another retired champion, John Jackson: 'have long lain the Amateurs under obligations which their subscriptions to his milling rooms do but faintly discharge. They have felt this some time; and a splendid service of plate is now preparing for him at Messrs. Clark, Cheapside.' The salver alone weighed 187 ounces, and the subscribers included the Duke of Clarence (later William IV), the Marquess of Worcester, Henry Smyth, Bart. MP, Admiral Tollemache and Major General Barton, all 'admirers of the gymnastic sports of their country'. It is to be doubted whether the presence of these representatives of the upper echelons caused the presentation dinner to be any less alcoholic or riotous than usual.

In the previous year, Jackson had supplied a force of prize-fighters 'to preserve order' during the coronation of George IV. A gold coronation medal was given to the boxers in recognition of their services, and a raffle of this trinket formed the excuse for yet another 'dinner' at which Tom Belcher drew the winning ticket.

Tom Belcher's more famous elder brother Jem had been less fortunate with the material gains of this life. Having resigned the championship following the loss of an eye, he unwisely returned to pugilism only to lose his unbeaten record and hard-earned cash to the formidable Hen Pearce. He then compounded his mistake by twice entering the ring with the heavier and fitter Tom Cribb, who brutally beat him on both occasions, but in his winning days Jem had gained immortality by wearing his fighting 'colours' tied in a certain stylish manner around his neck.

The wearing of colours by fighting men was a convention which can be traced back to the tournaments of the Middle Ages, where knights wore ladies handkerchiefs as a mark of favour. The practice had been revived by the early eighteenth century, as is proved in John Byrom's verses in praise of proto-pugilists Figg and Sutton:

> Their Arms were encircled by Armigers two,
> With a red Ribbon Sutton's and Figg's with a blue.

Blue was chosen by Tom Johnson, when in the 1780s he popularised the custom of displaying colours, tied both about the waist and to the corner posts of the boxing ring or stage. But it was Jem Belcher who raised the practice into the realms of high fashion at the beginning of the nineteenth century. Thereafter prize-fighters, coach-drivers, lords and even sporting parsons wore their neckties *à la Belcher*, the name at once passed into the English language and became synonymous with both necktie and handkerchief. Belcher's colours were originally yellow mixed with red and a little black, and this 'yellowman' became the symbol by which later fighters from Jem's native Bristol could be recognised. When Jem fought his

In the early part of the nineteenth century, the wearing of a 'Belcher' necktie became de rigueur *for all sportsmen, from the Corinthian lord down to the 'Bill Sykes' level of society. Fight promoter turned murderer John Thurtell even wore one to mount the scaffold, prior to being hanged outside Hertford Gaol in 1824.*
REPRODUCED BY COURTESY OF THE NATIONAL PORTRAIT GALLERY, LONDON.

fellow-townsman Hen Pearce 'The Game Chicken' in 1805, Pearce changed his colours to an appropriate birdseye blue, which as the mark of the winner on this occasion, coupled with the public's indelible association of victory with Jem, now also became known as a 'Belcher'. By the middle of the century 'Belcher' was the name applied to all spotted handkerchiefs, whatever their colour.

Although many fighters were to change their colours at random, some stuck to a favourite, especially when winning. Tom Spring, for instance, had a preference for either birdseye or plain blue. When Spring and Irish champion Jack Langan fought for the first time, their choice of colours, blue for Spring and black for Langan, occasioned much merriment from the Irishman's second Josh Hudson, who rather insensitively exclaimed: 'This is new, but nevertheless, the emblem is correct as to milling [laughing]; it is black and blue; I'll give a hundred to one, we shall see those colours upon their mugs before it is over.' He was right.

In 1823, whilst on a visit to his native place, after having beaten hard-hitting Bill Neat for the championship, Tom Spring, whose real name was Winter, was presented with a cup made from 3 lbs of silver by Messrs Grayhurst and Harvey of the Strand. This trophy, known as The Hereford Cup, bore an inscription surrounded by a device of apples: 'To Thomas Winter of Fownhope, in the county of Hereford, this cup was presented by his countrymen of the Land of Cider.' As if to further extol 'the wine of the country' the cup's lid even had a silver cider barrel as a finial, and, as the author of *Pugilistica* informs us, 'The inside is gilt; and it is large enough to hold a gallon of the "nectar divine".'

After Spring had defeated Jack Langan, he was presented with another cup. This time by a group of sportsmen from Manchester. The inscription praised Spring both as a fighter and as a private character, but this time rather carelessly omitted to mention cider or any other intoxicating liquor.

Both the 'Hereford' and 'Manchester' cups, together with snuff-boxes, canes, pencil cases and other prizes, were displayed on Spring's table at The Castle, Holborn, when in his retirement he was presented with:

> The third and most valuable public testimonial . . . . a noble tankard in silver, of the capacity of one gallon, or six bottles of wine, with a lining of 450 sovereigns, the balance of a subscription of over £500 raised by the ex-champion's friends. The tankard, which was executed by Messrs Hunt and Roskell, is a beautiful work of art, ornamented with chased bands of leaves of the British oak and English rose. The cover was surmounted by a bold acorn, the outer edge having in raised letters 'The Spring Testimonial'.

This presentation, accompanied by the now familiar 'excellent dinner', took place in 1846, by which time Ben Caunt and Bendigo were each commiting fouls to win or lose the championship and the prize-ring had fallen on evil times.

Old ring-followers were glad to look back to the palmy days of the 1820s and recall honest Tom in his prime. The Spring testimonial tankard bore the words: 'Presented by public subscription to Thomas Winter Spring, ex-Champion of England. In testimony of the sincere respect in which he is held for his pure and honourable conduct during his long and unblemished career in public and private life.'

Other fighters who did not hold the championship, but

whose honesty and integrity within the ring were highly esteemed, had also been presented with trophies of one kind or another back in the twenties. The unbeaten Jack Randall was given a pipe of wine worth £130, a gesture which showed a degree of foresight, insomuch as it forestalled the strong probability of any more lasting trophy being speedily converted into liquid comestables at the nearest pawnshop.

Ex-pawnbroker's assistant, Renton Nicholson, recounted the following unlikely story about a cup presented to Randall's friend and fellow-cockney, Josh Hudson, the popular 'John Bull Fighter':

An old friend of Josh's early days having, by reverse of fortune, by no means unfrequent among sporting men, fallen into a difficulty which called upon him for the immediate payment of some £50, applied in his extremity, to mine host of 'the Half Moon'. Josh, who had not the cash by him, was sadly annoyed at the idea of being compelled to refuse such an application from one from whom he had received favours.

A sudden thought struck him. There was his 'Cup', lying snug in its case in his iron safe. On that he could raise a temporary loan, and nobody the wiser. Desiring his friend to make himself at home while he went for 'the morpuses', Josh possessed himself of the piece of plate, hurried out at the side-door, and after a sharp toddle presented himself, blowing like a grampus, in one of the small boxes of a neighbouring 'Uncle' in Bishopsgate Street. Josh was not only a well-known public character, but it so happened that 'mine Uncle' was an admirer of the 'noble art'. Josh unlocked his box, and drew forth his well-earned trophy. The assistant eyed him with some curiosity.

'How much?'

'Forty pounds?' gasped Jolly Josh, not yet recovered from his run.

The assistant stepped into his employer's sanctum, who instantly returned with the shining pledge in his hands.

A brief colloquy explained the position of affairs. Josh wanted forty pounds.

'Mine Uncle' proceeded to his desk, but not to make out the 'ticket' required by law. He merely wrote an acknowledgement, to be signed by Josh, that he had received a loan of forty pounds. This 'mine Uncle' presented to him for signature. Josh was overwhelmed.

'No, no,' said mine Uncle! 'Take back your Cup, Josh, you must not be without it. Pay me, as I know you will, as soon as you are able. I'll not have that piece of wedge go to sale anyhow.' Josh returned to the Half Moon with both money and cup; discharged the duty of friendship, and the pawnbroker lost nothing by his confidence.

Hudson's cup had been awarded in 1823 to celebrate that boxer's unexpected win over up and coming Jem Ward. On the occasion of the dinner given to celebrate the presentation we are informed that 'the festive board was truly inviting; the wines excellent'; and the cup itself was 'filled with five bottles of port'. This trophy was heart-shaped, in allusion, it may be assumed, to Hudson's courage, rather than to the imminent cause of the self-indulgent pugilist's sudden demise at the age of thirty-eight.

Pierce Egan not only proposed and presented Hudson's cup, but composed the following doggerel and caused it to be engraved thereon:

> John Bull in the ring has so oft played his part,
> The form let it be in the shape of a heart –
> A true British one! at its shrine take a sup:
> Can a more noble model be found for a cup?

Egan was proud of his friendship with Hudson, and of his part in the production of the trophy. He introduced a visit to Josh's East End pub The Half-Moon Tap into *Finish to Life in London*, the sequel to the best-selling *Life in London*. In a scene strongly reminiscent of Tom and Jerry's earlier visit to Tom Cribb's parlour, the companions now admire Josh's cup and drink champagne from it, while a resident black boxer flourishes his fists and exclaims in stage patois, 'Me like a cup . . . a silver cup be a dam goot ting for massa. Must be a goot hit to make de cup by one blow. Me will hit 'em hard for a cup, when next me fights.' Yet, despite this spirited declaration of intent, there was to be no presentation of any sort of trophy to a black boxer until well into the Queensbury era.

Finish to Life in London appeared in instalments in 1827 and in July of that year Egan had advertised a 'Trip to the Nore,

In this Cruikshank engraving from Finish to Life in London, *Egan's crony Josh Hudson displays his trophies at the bar of the 'Half Moon Tap' in Leadenhall Market.*

accompanied by his pal Josh Hudson'. On this occasion the fighters' cup was exhibited on board, again brimming with port. When in the same year Mrs Hudson presented Josh with a son and heir, the fighter's friends and admirers saw fit, in a ceremony which foreshadowed the mawkish Cockney sentimentality of the succeeding age, to award young 'John Bull' his own little silver cup, inscribed: 'The gift of a few friends to Josh Hudson junior, born February 28th 1827, within the sound of Bow Bells.'

Although 'Champions' Cups' continued to be presented to and displayed by later claimants of the championship, including Ben Caunt, Bendigo, Tom Sayers and Jem Mace, they appear to have been awarded by admirers of the men in recognition of past services rather than representing any official acknowledgement of the titleholder. Current championship status, from the mid-1820s onwards, seems to have been more readily conveyed by a decorative belt, indeed by the middle of the century 'The Championship' and 'The Belt' had become synonymous.

The earliest recorded instance of a belt being awarded as the result of a specific championship fight was in 1825, after Jem Ward had defeated Tom Cannon. This prototype championship belt was assembled from the blue and crimson colours worn during the fight, and bound with tiger skin. The buckle was made of highly polished steel encircled with 'emblematical' designs, and in the middle was a heart, worked with gold, on which was engraved: 'This belt was presented to James Ward, in commemoration of his scientific and manly conquest of Thomas Cannon . . . This battle, at the present time, entitles him to the high and distinquished appellation of the British Champion.' Jem had scarcely put the belt on when he said with a smile: 'I have got it, and I mean to keep it.'

Keep it he certainly did, for there is no mention of any handing over of the trophy when he was defeated by Peter Crawley eighteen months later. Crawley immediately retired, Ward reassumed the title of Champion, and, upon beating Simon Byrne in 1831, was presented with a second belt by no less an authority than Tom Spring himself. This really does seem to have been recognised as the *bona fide* championship insignia, for the following year *Bell's Life in London* published a letter in which Ward stated that he had taken the 'Belt' public house in Liverpool, that it was his intention to retire from the ring, and to hand over the champion's belt to the first man who proved himself worthy of it.

'Deaf' Burke surely proved worthy when in 1833 he defeated Simon Byrne after the most protracted and brutal of championship fights, but Ward, who acted as second to the losing man, refused to acknowledge the winner's claim. So the trophy remained in the possession of its original owner for the following six years during which period 'The Deaf 'Un' claimed the championship. Finally, a sadly out of condition Burke head-butted Bendigo in frustration during their brief title fight and Ward's younger brother Nick, was on hand to shout 'foul'.

Jem Ward then presented the belt to Bendigo despite that gentleman's defeat at the hands of Ben Caunt in the previous year. It would be interesting to know what grudge the Ward brothers held against their fellow-East Ender 'Deaf' Burke; suffice it to say that the only belt that the Deaf 'Un ever owned was that which secured a truss worn in consequence of a rupture. This harmless support Bendigo and his party insisted should be removed before the commencement of the contest, an extremely unsporting tactic of which Burke complained greviously, but to no avail.

Bendigo and Caunt now both claimed the championship but Bendigo held the belt, and Caunt then lost his share of the championship to Nick Ward on yet another disputable foul.

While Caunt and Ward junior were in training for a return fight in 1841 a subscription was raised to produce a new Champion's Belt, to be presented to the victor of the forth-coming event, and to be thereafter transferable should he retire or be beaten.

The new belt was exhibited in the ring immediately before the fight:

> It is composed of purple velvet, and lined with leather; in the centre are a pair of clasped hands surrounded by a wreath of the Rose, the Thistle, and the Shamrock, en-twined in embossed silver; on each side of this are three shields of bright silver [on which] are to be engraven the names of all the Champions of England . . . to conclude with the name of the conqueror on the present occasion. The clasps in front are formed of two hands encased in sparring-gloves . . . Caunt, on taking it in his hand, signi-ficantly said to Nick Ward, 'This is mine, Nick,' to which Ward replied, 'I hope the best man may win it and wear it.'

Thirty-five rounds proved Caunt to be the best man; accord-ingly, he was proclaimed champion and the official trophy was buckled around his waist. A novel sequel to this ceremony took place when, upon the winner's return to London after the fight, 'he was presented with a pair of braces, manufactured by the fair hand of a lady, on which, in anticipation of the result, were inscribed the words "Benjamin Caunt, Champion of England, 11th May, 1841"'.

Within four months Ben had sailed for America, taking the belt, and presumably the braces, with him. Caunt's belt seems to have been regarded as the genuine article, for when in 1845 following his return to England, Ben was declared to have lost the championship for incautiously sitting down during the

93rd round of his third match with Bendigo, the official insignia was handed to his 'conqueror'.

Little more is heard about official belts until five years later when Bill Perry, 'The Tipton Slasher', having beaten all and sundry, demanded that Bendigo should hand over the belt or come out of retirement and fight for it. The shifty Bendigo wisely declined the challenge but stated that the belt had been presented to him as a gift or testimonial, and was his own property.

So matters stood until 1855 when 'a proposition was set on foot . . . to raise, by subscription, a sum of money to purchase a belt of greater intrinsic value than anything of the kind previously presented, in lieu of the belt which had "gone astray". . . . A sum of nearly £100 was collected. To Mr Hancock, of New Bond Street, was entrusted the manufacture of the trophy.'

This new belt consisted of seven solid silver plaques joined together with silver hinges in the form of ropes. On each panel were rather coarse but charmingly modelled scenes. The centre panel carried a Royal Coat of Arms in relief. On that to the right were engraved the words CHAMPION OF ENGLAND, whilst to the left was a blank shield ready to receive the name of the first outright winner. The panels to either side of these displayed pugilists in attitude, and the final scenes were a pair of clasped hands and a British lion couchant.

On the belt being ordered the committee who undertook its management issued the following conditions on which it was to be held:

> That it should not be handed over to any person claiming the Championship until he had proved his right to it by a fight; that any pugilist having held it against all-comers for three years, without a defeat, should become its absolute possessor; that the holder should be bound to meet every challenger of any weight who should challenge him for the sum of £200 a side . . .; that at the final deposit for every match within the three years the belt should be delivered up to the committee until after the battle; and finally, that on the belt being given to the winner of any Champion-fight, he should deposit such security as should be deemed necessary in the hands of the committee to ensure the above regulations being carried out.

On 22 June 1857 the new belt was clasped around the waist of Tom Sayers, who within a week previously had cut to ribbons the face of the once formidable 'Tipton Slasher'.

One year to the day after defeating the 'Slasher', Sayers disposed of Tom Paddock who had also laid claim to the championship. On this occasion, in addition to retaining the belt, Sayers was presented with the cup and belt made for

Tom Cribb almost half a century earlier, in recognition of having finally ended the years of wrangling, by becoming undisputed champion.

Sayers was to follow up these successes with more victories and had looked like making the belt his own property when a challenge was received from across the Atlantic.

Volumes have been written describing how on 17 April 1860 in a field at Farnborough, Hampshire, Sayers with a severely disabled right arm, and the blinded American John Camel Heenan shared the honours at the end of forty-two rounds, occupying two hours and twenty minutes. And how after much argument, it was finally agreed by all parties that each man had thoroughly earned the Championship and that both were to be presented with an exact replica of the Champion's belt.

The presentation ceremony took place on 30 May, and was fully reported in the next morning's edition of *The Times*:

> The differences between the rival champions, Sayers and Heenan, were brought to an amicable termination last evening, when a silver belt, of precisely the same make and value, was formally presented to each of the great pugilists. The interesting ceremony . . . took place in the Alhambra Palace, Leicester Square, in the presence of many patrons of the 'noble art'. . . . The belts, the coveted recompense of such matchless skill and endurance, lay upon a table in the centre of the arena, the winners and their friends being grouped around them. Before the addresses were delivered which were to precede the award, the pugilists advanced half-way towards each other, and cordially shook hands in token of their final reconciliation. The first belt of the two was presented to Heenan, accompanied by an address written on parchment, which was formally read amid the vociferous cheering of the concourse by Mr Dowling.

There followed a verbose oration in praise of Heenan, by the editor of *Bell's Life in London*, after which:

> The belt, a massive piece of silver, about three inches in width, bearing the inscription 'Champion of England', and ornamented with several designs emblematical of the prize-ring, was then handed to Heenan, who straitway buckled it round his waist, amid loud and prolonged applause.
>
> Then came Sayers' turn to receive his hard-earned decoration. The éloge of England's Champion, in keeping with the chivalric courtesies of the occasion, was pronounced by Mr Wilkes, Editor of the New York *Spirit of the Times*. Mr Wilkes' somewhat florid sentences were delivered in a tone of much solemnity and with deep feeling . . .
>
> The reading of this address was frequently interrupted by

THE CHAMPION'S BELT.

vehement cheering; but a passage alluding to its having been Heenan's generous intention to return *the* belt to Sayers, if he had been fortunate enough to win it from him at Farnborough, was received with very significant murmurs. Poor Sayers, the blushing object of Mr Wilkes' glowing periods, seemed hardly to know what to make of all the high-flown compliments so liberally lavished upon him; and when the 'shining girdle' was passed to him with the injunction to 'buckle it about his loins', he seized it with an apparent sense of relief, and immediately fastened it around him. The awkwardness he displayed in this operation owing to the cumbrous make of the belt and the difficulty of fitting it to his waist, provoked mingled laughter and cheers. The oratory was, however, not yet finished. Mr Wilkes, still addressing the puzzled Sayers, said he had still one part, and perhaps not the least significant part, of his duty to perform, and that was to return him the 'battle money', which he had never lost. Tom again held out his hand to receive this tangible recognition of his unconquered prowess – a portion of the ceremony which was certainly fully as intelligible to him as the rest of the flattering ovation. The champions, arrayed in their 'glittering testimonials' –

Sayers and Heenan each receive identical championship belts during an absurd ceremony held at the Alhambra Palace, London, one month after their drawn fight. Heenan's belt is now in the possession of the British Boxing Board of Control.
REPRODUCED BY COURTESY OF THE MANSELL COLLECTION.

then walked arm in arm round the arena for a few moments, to exhibit themselves to the spectators. While this was going on few could refrain from remarking the wonderful disparity in the size and stature of the two men, the huge 'boy' having to stoop and walk in an ungainly attitude in order to keep step with his comparatively diminutive companion . . .

Having sufficiently gratified their audience with a sight of them, the friendly athletes next acknowledged the honours that had been paid them. Their oratory might serve as models of brevity and pith. The Benicia Boy contented himself with assuring his friends that that was the happiest moment of his life; and Tom Sayers, in turn, said he 'followed in his comrade's wake', and was much obliged to them all . . . The ceremony of the presentation is to be repeated at the same place today, Friday, and Saturday.

The humour of the occasion seems to have been lost upon the author of *Pugilistica*, who declined to record the ceremony, with the exclamation that: '. . . the whole affair, speeches and all, savour too strongly of the circus style of bunkum and bombast.' Instead he confined himself to quoting a rather more prosaic paragraph from the previous day's edition of *The Times*, the writer of which concluded by stating:

We have been favoured with a view of the old belt, 'the belt' still open to competition, and of the two other belts to be presented to the 'two Champions of England', for such is the inscription upon the case of each. Both are precisely similar in every respect, and the somewhat clumsy workmanship, in frosted silver, carefully copied from the original, is by Mr C. F. Hancock, of Bruton Street.

Heenan now departed to his native land, while Sayers retired from the ring to display his trophy throughout England and to receive the plaudits of the populace. During the following year there were many rumours of Heenan returning to England to claim the Championship from Sam Hurst, the current holder of the 1855 belt, but nothing came of this 'newspaper talk'.

However, in the spring of 1862, Heenan, as one American newspaper put it, had 'gone over [to England] to fetch the old belt, and to fight Mace, the so-called Champion'. But Jem Mace, who had earlier relieved Hurst of the belt, was to lose it to Tom King at the end of the year. Heenan had to wait another twelve months before arrangements to fight King were concluded; the American was then defeated in thirty-five minutes and his conqueror retired with the prize money of £2,000, leaving the original belt to Mace who 'resumed the style of "Champion"', with whatever honours might still attach to that 'tarnished title'. Very few honours and even less money attached to what had by this time become a very tarnished title indeed.

Jem Mace was to make the 1855 belt his own property, with two rather one-sided defeats of Joe Goss. Following the second of these victories in 1866, the short-lived *Illustrated Sporting News* presented Mace with an additional rather handsome velvet and silver belt. As we shall see, Jem Mace seems to have started a fashion among pugilists for collecting various belts which had no relevance to any specific title or championship.

Meanwhile, one Joe Wormald had been invested with Heenan's belt upon defeating the even more obscure Andrew Marsden for 'the championship' in 1865.

Amid the pugilistic confusion of the mid-sixties, a new age had been heralded by the publication in 1867 of the Marquis of Queensbury's Rules, and the presentation by the Marquis of silver cups for Heavy, Middle and Lightweight competition to the newly formed Amateur Boxing Club. Jem Mace, sensing the wind of change, sailed for America, and by the end of the decade, Wormald, Goss, and most of the remnants of the English prize-ring had also crossed to the New World.

Mace had hardly set foot in America when he was challenged by fellow-Englishman, Tom Allen, who had dubbed himself Champion of America. Jem's written reply contained the following paragraph: 'In reference to the belt, which you say is shortly to be presented to you, I wish to say that my

The 'colours' used by Jem Mace, presumably before losing his championship in 1862, to Tom King, who is shown in the border as one of Mace's victims (Mace had beaten King earlier in the same year). The shield in each corner is that of Norwich, the county town of the fighter's native Norfolk.

friends in New York propose to present me with a belt also, which I will put up against yours and contest for in addition to the stakes.' It is not clear what either of these belts was actually presented for, but we may assume that they were both transferred to Mace upon his easy conquest of Allen at New Orleans in 1870, after which Jem assumed the title 'Champion of the World'.

The bare-knuckle game had definitely passed to America, where nothing more is heard about championship belts or cups for another fourteen years.

Then in 1884, with two rival champions in the field, but without a blow being struck, Richard K. Fox, proprietor of the New York based *Police Gazette*, presented *his* champion, Irish-born Jake Kilrain, with a solid gold and silver 'championship' belt, weighing 200 ounces, and 'of far greater inherent value than any trophy hitherto connected with the prize-ring'. Incensed, the citizens of Boston collected $10,000 and purchased for their 'champion', John L. Sullivan, his own personal belt of solid gold, studded with 397 diamonds. Sullivan, upon being invested with this gaudy bauble in 1887, contemptuously dimissed *The Police Gazette* belt as 'just a dog collar'.

In the same year Kilrain and British Champion Jem Smith fought a 106-round contest for the 'championship of the world' and *The Police Gazette* belt. This epic fight which took place in France, was declared a draw when darkness fell, so

Richard K. Fox of the New York based Police Gazette, *presented this 'World Championship' belt to his protégé Jake Kilrain in 1884, by which time the USA had become the virtual home of prize-fighting.*

the Irish-American kept the belt and his version of the championship.

Eventually in 1889, amid unprecedented ballyhoo, Sullivan and Kilrain met at Richburg, Mississippi, for what was destined to be the final bare-knuckle championship contest ever staged. After seventy-five rounds, lasting two hours and sixteen minutes, Sullivan was declared 'champion of the world'; he then had *The Police Gazette* 'dog collar' valued at $175 and dismissed it back to Fox. As for the belt presented by the good people of Boston, it travelled back and fourth to the pawn shop with astounding regularity, and was still good for credit even after Sullivan had removed all 397 diamonds to settle his more pressing drink bills.

Although in England the prize-ring had been all but dead since the mid-sixties, the last bare-knuckle title fight on British soil took place as late as 1885, when Jem Smith knocked out one Jack Davis in just eight minutes. But it is far from certain whether a belt or any other memento was awarded to mark the occasion. What is clear is that in the preceding twenty or so years British society had changed almost beyond recognition, and that during the 1880s, a decade which culminated in Queen Victoria's Silver Jubilee, very few people of influence or of even common decency would have countenanced a prize-fight, much less contributed to any sort of trophy for the winner.

Belts presented by the National Sporting Club, which were later known as 'Lonsdale' belts, did not make an appearance until 1909, and were then, of course, awarded to winners of British championship bouts, governed by 'Queensbury Rules' and involving gloves, timed rounds and the possibility of victory on points. What a contrast with 1865, when, following the melancholy death of Tom Sayers, *The Times* had seen fit to publish the following list of items from a sale of the late champion's effects:

Lot 13. Solid gold 'Cross of Valour', . . . presented by the officers of Her Majesty's ship *Malborough* (2 oz 1 dwt) £10.10s.

Lot 14. A solid gold medal presented by a few friends in New York for gallantry while defending the 'Belt'. £8.5s.

Lot 15. A silver medal 'Model of Prize-ring' presented for bravery and endurance at Farnborough. £4.

Lot 24. A silver cigar-case, richly ornamented (7 oz 6 dwt). £7.7s.

Lot 25. A silver pint tankard presented . . . 'for bravery and skill' (10 oz 19 dwt). £9.

Lot 26. A hunt cup presented for 'manly conduct in and out of the Ring'. (11 oz 18 dwt). £10.

Lot 27. A silver cup presented as a token of manly courage on April 17, 1860. (11 oz). £9.9s.

Lot 28. A silver cup, with two handles, by Hunt and Roskell, presented to the late Champion by Captain Webster for his gallant conduct on the occasion of his fight, in 1857, with Aaron Jones; this was a really beautiful article, it weighed 19 oz. 13 dwts, and bore on the obverse side the

A woven silk 'Stevengraph' of c1887, depicting British champion Jem Smith, who wears Union Jack colours around his waist, rather than the championship belt to which he was undoubtably entitled.

quotation, 'Courage, fight it out! A crown or a glorious tomb!' It was knocked down for £31.10s.

Lot 29. A two-handled silver cup, the gift of Mr. T. Foreman, for 'gallant conduct in his late encounter – Farnborough' (34 oz 10 dwts). £27.6s.

Lot 30. A silver wine tankard, the present of a few friends at Montreal, June 1860 (25 oz 10 dwts). £17.7s.6d.

Lot 31. Tom Cribb's Champion Cup (76 oz 10 dwts). £35.

Lot 33. The Champion Belt, presented on the occasion of the International Prizefight, . . . by Mr. Wilkes of New York. £38.12s.

Lot 34. Tom Cribb's Championship Belt. £18.10s.

This list and the fact that the quality press had deigned to notice it, gives some indication of the esteem in which the hero of Farnborough and his profession had been held by many members of the upper, as well as the lower orders of mid-Victorian society.

In a lithograph published by George Webb of London in 1860, the well-fed Tom Sayers exhibits his hard-won trophies, including the large cup and lion-skin belt made for Tom Cribb, half a century earlier.

BOXIANA;

OR, Sketches OF

Antient & Modern

PUGILISM.

LONDON.

Published by G. SMEETON, 139, S. Martin's Lane, Charing Cross.

JULY, 1812.

CHAPTER 6

SCRIBES AND CHRONICLERS

Yesterday a match of Boxing was performed before His Grace the Duke of Albemarle, between the Duke's footman and a butcher. The latter won the prize, as he hath done many before, being accounted, though but a little man, the best at that exercise in England.

THE *PROTESTANT MERCURY*, JANUARY 1681

Title page from the first volume of Boxiana, *published in 1812. Mendoza and Humphries are depicted 'in attitude' after a painting by Charles Ryley. The classical poses of the rival pugilists in this engraving, in turn, inspired Theodore Géricault's 'Boxeurs'.*

Newspaper reports of boxing matches were to appear with increasing frequency during the years which followed the *Protestant Mercury*'s much quoted first announcement, until by the middle of the eighteenth century pugilistic journalism had become an integral part of the English way of life, with regular reports in such popular papers as the *Gentleman's Magazine*, the *Flying Post*, the *Daily News Letter* and the *World*.

Then in about 1740, at a time when pugilism had scaled new heights of popularity with the advent of Jack Broughton and his school, there appeared Captain Godfrey's splendid volume, *A Treatise on the Useful Art of Self-Defence*, the first publication to deal at any length with the current craze for fisticuffs. Besides presenting vigorous first-hand word portraits of both Broughton and Figg together with their contemporaries, the *Treatise* also contains the earliest full descriptions of pugilistic encounters and their preliminaries to appear since Roman times. The first contest to be detailed is one which had taken place in 1733 between Bob Whitaker, a regular member of Figg's troupe, and a giant Venetian gondolier. Godfrey takes up the story:

I was at Slaughter's Coffee-house when the match was made by a gentleman of advanced station: he sent for Fig to procure a proper man for him. He told him to take care of the man, because it was for a large sum; and the Venetian was of wonderful strength, and famous for breaking the jawbone in boxing. Fig replied, in his rough manner, 'I do not know, master, but he may break one of his countryman's jawbones with his fist; but I'll bring him a man, and he shall not be able to break his jawbone with a sledgehammer.'

The battle was fought at Fig's amphitheatre, before a splendid company, the politest house of that kind I ever saw. While the Gondolier was stripping my heart yearned for my countryman. His arm took up all observation; it was surprisingly large, long, and muscular. He pitched himself forward with his right leg, and his arm full extended; and, as Whitaker approached, caught him a blow at the side of the head which knocked him quite off stage, which was remarkable for its height. Whitaker's misfortune in his fall was the grandeur of the company, on which account they suffered no common people in, that usually sat on the ground, and lined the stage all round. It was thus all clear, and Whitaker had nothing to stop him but the bottom. There was a general foreign huzza on the side of the Venetian, as proclaiming our countryman's downfall; but Whitaker took no more time than was required to get up again, when, finding his fault in standing out to the length of the other's arm, he, with a little stoop, dashed boldly in beyond the heavy mallet, and with one English peg in the stomach, quite a new thing to foreigners, brought him on his breech. The blow carried too much of the English rudeness with it for him to bear, and finding himself so unmannerly used, he scorned to have any more doings with such a slovenly fist.

The Captain continues:

So fine a house was too engaging to Fig not to court another. He therefore stepped up, and told the gentleman that they might think he had picked the best man in London on this occasion; but to convince them to the contrary, he said, that if they would come on that day se'night, he would bring a man who should beat this Whitaker in ten minutes by fair hitting. This brought near as great and fine a company as the week before. The 'man' was Nathaniel Peartree, who, knowing the other's bottom, and his deadly way of flinging, took a most judicious manner to beat him. He . . . cunningly determined to fight at his eyes. His judgement carried his arm so well, that, in about six minutes, both Whitaker's eyes were shut; when, groping about a while for his man, and finding him not, he wisely gave out, with these odd words; 'Damme, I'm not beat; but what signifies my fighting when I can't see my man?'

Here, in an episode which exactly foreshadowed the blinding, seventeen years later, of Broughton by Jack Slack, we can already recognise many of the elements of modern fight-promotion and match-making. Brash challenges and counter-claims, combined with a well-appointed and conveniently sited arena, served then no less than now to draw a large and knowledgeable crowd of paying spectators. Then, when a brave and skilful native beats a huge and formidable foreigner in a contest complemented by a thrilling 'boxer versus fighter' sequel, the climax of which is as sudden as it is unexpected, the spectators are delighted and will pay to see more.

Whereas Godfrey's *Treatise*, dedicated to HRH The Duke of Cumberland and to be found in the Royal Library at Windsor, had catered in common with journals such as the *Gentleman's Magazine* for the taste of an upper and middle-class readership, there appeared during the second half of the eighteenth century a rash of cheap leaflets and chap-books aimed at a newly literate boxing public. Hurriedly written and crudely printed, these charming examples of early street literature were issued under the name of any popular boxer of the time who happened to take the publisher's fancy, the boxers themselves having little or nothing whatever to do with, and drawing no revenue from, the publications which so freely and arbitrarily bore their names. It is interesting to note that the practice continued well into the next century with such titles as *Owen Swift's Handbook of Boxing*, published in 1840. Popular on both sides of the Atlantic, this slim manual was in fact written by the disreputable showman Renton Nicholson, a personal friend of Swift's, so it is to be hoped that the great little boxer at least gained some remuneration from the venture.

How much of a hand Daniel Mendoza had in writing *The Art of Boxing*, which bears his name and was published in about 1790 while the champion of Jewry was at the pinnacle of his career, must remain a matter of conjecture, although it would seem that such an undertaking was not beyond his considerable capabilities. Apart from its claim to be the first publication actually written by a boxer, Mendoza's rare volume is most valuable and interesting in that it describes, in some detail, both the purported author's method of fighting and the recommended training regimen current at the time of the prize-ring's ascendancy to the position of a national sport.

A quarter of a century later Mendoza, down on his luck, and ever ready to earn an honest penny, was to publish his memoirs. In this highly entertaining little book the fifty-two-year-old ex-champion sketches his East End childhood and early career, before describing at length his rise to fame attendant upon the battles, both in and out of the ring, with Dick Humphries. Throughout the *Memoirs* Mendoza sees himself through rose-tinted spectacles: the numerous youthful street fights and consequent loss of employment are never *his* fault; he is merely protecting the weak, or avenging an insult. He gains and loses several fortunes, and during his years of affluence rides to hounds with noblemen, is backed by the Prince of Wales and is even presented to the King, the first Jew to be accorded such an honour. Thoroughgoing Israelite that he is, one of the chief concerns is always the acquisition of

The surprise defeat of Broughton by Slack in 1750. This engraving from Lord Byron's screen is probably by Hogarth, who certainly seems to have witnessed the contest. Around the edges may be seen some of the pugilistic press cuttings with which the poet filled any spaces between illustrations.

REPRODUCED BY COURTESY OF JOHN MURRAY LTD.

what he considers to be his due, whether gate money, prize money or royal handouts. Ultimately, however, he shows a lack of business acumen more usually associated with the boxer than with the Levantine, and by the time of writing his memoirs he is back in Whitechapel where he started – broke! As with *The Art of Boxing*, it is far from clear how much of the *Memoirs* is actually from the pen of the pugilist, but with its extreme if amusing egotism and self-righteousness, it certainly has about it the ring of authentic autobiography.

In 1792 the newly founded *Sporting Magazine* had published the first history of boxing. This undertaking, issued in monthly instalments, was composed largely in response to the tremendous amount of public interest aroused by the bitter rivalry between Mendoza and Humphries. At the same time as producing some of the earliest fight reports to appear in *The Times*, the Mendoza and Humphries feud was to generate as large a boom in sporting literature as it had with popular engravings or commemorative ceramics. In this it foreshadowed the even greater bulk of graphic material of all kinds, stimulated by the violently nationalistic Cribb versus Molineaux epics of twenty years later.

In addition to the by now regular newspaper reports, the first few years of the nineteenth century were to see the publication of some anonymously written 'recollections' of pugilism. Then in 1811, following Cribb's initial victory over Molineaux, more books began to appear, catering to an ever-increasing public demand for prize-ring reports and history. The first of these publications was called *Lives of the Boxers* and was written by one Jonathan Badcock, who quite understandably preferred to be known by his *nom de plume* of Jon Bee. This highly eccentric and unstable character also claimed to have written the other major pugilistic presentation of 1811, *Pancratia: A History of Boxing*, although it is more generally and believably credited to the pen of fight-following comic actor Bill Oxberry.

Pancratia was published by the well-known London firm of George Smeeton, which in the next year brought out the grandiosely entitled best-seller: *Boxiana: or Sketches of Ancient and Modern Pugilism; from the days of the renowned Broughton and Slack, to the heroes of the present milling Æra!* 'by one of the Fancy'. *Boxiana* took the sporting world by storm, completely surpassing everything that had gone before. 'One of the Fancy' then revealed himself to be none other than Pierce Egan, at that time an employee of Smeeton. Jon Bee later disputed Egan's claim, stating that the idea had been stolen from *his Pancratia*, and that the offending author was Joseph Smeeton. Unfortunately for Bee's argument, Smeeton had been dead for three years by the time of publication.

During the next three decades Egan's name was to become almost synonymous with the prize-ring, enormously popular

George Sharples here portrays Pierce Egan 'togged in two-pen'north of decency' complete with 'Belcher Fogle round the squeeze'. We have the writer's own word that he more usually resembled 'the rough hedgehog, with a beard of nearly four days' growth – a waistcoat which had seen much better days . . . aged pantaloons that would have puzzled any draper as to their original colour – a coat or rather part of one . . . reduced to a thread-bare remnant – and with slippers to correspond . . .'

and widely read in his time; today he is largely forgotten. Even the circumstances surrounding his birth are obscure, but we do know that he was the son of an immigrant Irish labourer, and that he was born in about 1774, in either Ireland or London. Growing up in Holborn, Egan combined, to an extreme degree, the chirpiness of the Cockney with an inherent Hibernian wit.

Having served at least part of a printing apprenticeship, young Pierce was soon earning his living as a contributor of sporting articles to various newspapers and periodicals. The meagre income of a Grub Street journalist was supplemented by work as a parliamentary reporter, for which Egan, like the young Charles Dickens, taught himself shorthand, which was later to stand him in such good stead amidst the noise and bustle at ringside.

Boxiana was produced largely as a celebration of Tom Cribb's second victory over Molineaux in 1811, and Egan's description of the contest is a classic example of the author's relatively plain early style. The proliferation of capital letters and italics, together with highly eccentric punctuation, are all indispensible hallmarks of Egan's writing:

Never was the *sporting world* so much interested, and for twenty miles within the seat of action not a bed could be obtained on the preceding night: and by six o'clock the next morning, hundreds were in motion to get a good place near the stage, which even at that early period proved a difficult task. It is supposed that near 20,000 persons witnessed this tremendous *mill*: and that one-fourth of them were of the *highest mould*, including some of the principal CORINTHIANS of the state. VICTORY proving so long doubtful in the former combat, rendered the capabilities of the MOOR, an object of fear and jealousy, on the part of the friends of the CHAMPION, who viewed him as a rival of the most daring quality: and *one* not to be disposed of with the common routine of *punishment*. They neither of them weighed so much as in the last fight by a stone; and CAPTAIN BARCLAY whose knowledge of the capacity of the human frame appears to be better than most men, took the CHAMPION under his immediate eye, and trained him upon a system peculiar to himself, reducing CRIB from upwards of sixteen stone, to about thirteen stone six pounds, yet kept his stamina unimpaired. From such patronage and protection the bets were three to one on the CHAMPION; and six to four that he gave the first knock down blow.

A few minutes after twelve o'clock, they mounted the stage (25 feet) CRIB springing upon it with great confidence and bowing to the spectators. The applause exceeded every thing of the kind: the *Moor* followed and jumped over the railing with considerable spirit, bowing, and was greeted with tokens of approbation, though not of so general a nature. Both the combatants looked well; and *Molineaux*, for a man of colour, might be termed rather good-looking: but CRIB appearing to have the longest arms. The *Moor* appeared disturbed and walked the stage with hasty steps. On stripping, the anxiety of the multitude cannot be described; and they were soon brought to the mark by their seconds, *Gully* and *Joe Ward* for CRIB, and *Richmond* and *Bill Gibbons*, for *Molineaux*:

First round – A minute elapsed in sparring, when the CHAMPION made play right and left, and put in a right-handed blow on the body of the *Moor*, who returned a feeble hit on his opponents *nob*. A rally now commenced, in which a few blows were exchanged, and *Molineaux* received a hit in his throat, which sent him down, though not considered clean.

Second – The *claret* was perceived to issue first from the mouth of CRIB, upon commencing this round. A most

'Tom Cribb, Engraved by Jn Young, Engraver in Mezzotint to HRH The Prince Regent. From the original picture by Douglas Guest Esq. In possession of Sir Henry Smyth Bart.' This portrait of Cribb was commissioned by the boxer's leading patron, following the champion's first defeat of Molineaux in 1810.

A fold-out engraving of Cribb v. *Molineaux from* Boxiana. *The crudely drawn figures are both based upon well-known mezzotints by John Young, from paintings by the accomplished Douglas Guest.*

terrible rally took place by mutual consent, when the CHAMPION planted with his right hand a severe body hit, which was returned on the head by *Molineaux*, with his left flush. They both fought at half-arm's-length for superiority, and about six good hits were exchanged, when they closed, and in a trial of strength, CRIB was thrown. Five to two on the CHAMPION.

Cribb's right eye had been completely closed in the final stages of round two, while his opponent was already badly short of breath. So, although the odds at one point got down to seven-to-four on Cribb, the damage remained fairly evenly distributed until in the sixth round:

Molineaux from want of wind, lunged right and left, but gained nothing by it, and stopped with neatness the right hand of the Champion. CRIB now gave the *Moor* so severe a blow in the body with his right hand, that it not only appeared to *roll him up*, but seemed as if he had completely knocked the wind out of him, which issued so strong from his mouth like smoke from a pipe, that he was literally gasping for breath. On renewing a rally, he behaved quite frantic, and seemed bewildered as to what manner he should conduct himself – afraid of his opponent's *punishment*, he dared not go in although wishing so to do, and capered about in an extravagant manner, to the derision of CRIB and the spectators, hit short and was quite abroad; when the CHAMPION pursued him round the stage with great success, and concluded the round by a full-length hit, which laid the *Moor* prostrate. Five to one on CRIB.

The Englishman now had the fight all his own way and by round nine:

It was so evident which way the battle would now terminate, that it was '*Lombard Street to a China Orange,*' CRIB was the conqueror. The *Moor* in running in, had his jaw broke, and fell as if dead, from a tremendous left-handed blow from the Champion. *Molineaux* did not come to his time by a full half a minute – but CRIB wished that the spectators should fully witness his superiority in giving away his *chance* – dancing about the stage, when he ought to have been proclaimed the conqueror; and went in again, knocking him nearly down, and then up again, and *levelled* him.

Poor Molineaux was brought up to receive unnecessary punishment for two more rounds, before being knocked unconscious, to the undisguised delight of the partisan crowd. Egan then summed up:

It appeared in the above BATTLE, that the *Moor* had acquired *science* equal to the CHAMPION, and was viewed as a good *in-fighter*; remarkably quick and weighty with his left hand, and who returned on his opponent's *head*, whenever he received in the body: but no question now remains concerning the superiority of the combatants – CRIB having won a main, and beat the *Moor* in *nineteen minutes and ten seconds*, when in the former battle, it continued thrice the duration: which can only be accounted for, that CRIB was too full of flesh in that combat, and not in good condition; and *Molineaux* had improved respecting *science*, but injured his stamina. The hardest frame could not resist the blows of the *Champion*; and it is astonishing the *Moor* stood them so long. He was taken out of the ring senseless and could not articulate; and it was thought upon the first examination that his jaw-bone and two of his ribs were fractured: while on the contrary, CRIB scarcely received a body blow, but his head was terribly out of shape . . . All the towns upon the North road gained considerably by this contest . . . Among the company who witnessed the battle, were the Marquess of Queensbury, Sir Henry Smyth, Lord Yarmouth, the Hon. Berkeley Craven, Major Mellish, Captain Barclay, General Grosvenor, Lord Pomfret, Sir Francis Baynton, Sir Charles Alton, Thomas Goddard, Esq., Mr. Gorè, &c. &c. and all the sporting amateurs and professors in the kingdom.

With its vigorous round-by-round descriptions of fights, detailed biographies of fighters, encyclopaedic inside knowledge and copious use of what the author would have termed 'flash' sporting slang, *Boxiana* was to become the virtual Bible of the boxing fraternity. Egan followed up his initial success with a second volume in 1818, published by Sherwood, Neely and Jones, who also reissued Volume 1 in the same year. Then after Volume 3 had appeared in 1821, Egan quarrelled with his new publisher, who in 1824 employed the by now insanely jealous Jon Bee to compile Volume 4, a task which it must be said he accomplished magnificently, though in a style which owed much to the original author. Egan then turned to the well-known publisher George Virtue for the final two volumes of 1828 and 1829, which are confusingly known as Volumes 1 and 2 of the 'New Series'. Taken together, the total of six books brilliantly chronicle the history of the prize-ring and the careers of its leading exponents throughout English pugilism's golden age.

Egan is writing for the well-heeled 'Corinthians', whom he described lounging at ring-side. He even goes so far as to dedicate *Boxiana* to selected members of the sporting gentry and nobility. Beginning in Volume 1 with Cribb's trainer and backer, Captain Barclay, the dedications ascend through the ranks of the peerage until they reach a climax in the final edition with no less a supporter of pugnacity than the Duke of Wellington!

We know that, at the top end of the social scale, the sport was keenly followed in the public schools; indeed, Egan himself informs us 'without fear of contradiction' that he furnished the Duke of Buccleuch with all the volumes of *Boxiana*, in addition to boxing gloves during that nobleman's sojourn at Eton, and a browse through *Tom Brown's Schooldays* clearly demonstrates that the pupils of Rugby School in no way lagged behind their southern counterparts in an appreciation of 'The Noble Art'.

An affluent readership is pre-supposed by the price of 16–18 shillings per volume, which, combined with the fact that each book contains in excess of 140,000 words, effectively ruled out the poor and uneducated masses, the majority of whom were to remain in ignorance of letters until after the Elementary Education Act of 1870.

Most fighters came from, and remained members of, the unlettered classes, unable even to sign their names at the foot of fight articles. There were of course a few exceptions, like John Jackson, some of whose well-written letters are still extant. The accomplished Mr Jackson could not only write, but, as Egan tells us, could do so with an 84lb. weight suspended from his little finger! John Gully, in addition to being a financial genius, was also highly literate and his stylish signature is to be found on a variety of documents from his later careers on the turf and in Parliament.

Egan often tried rather unconvincingly to insert 'proofs' of literacy and even gentility into the biographies of certain favoured fighters, as for instance when he informs us that Bob Gregson, 'Poet Laureate to the heroic race of pugilists', 'was descended from very respectable parents, who possessed a farm of considerable extent . . . Bob's education was by no means neglected; and he . . . was allied by marriage to a family of some importance . . .' At which point the author of *Pugilistica*, unable any longer to contain himself, was to add the snide comment, 'We have Egan's word for it, who doubtless had it from Bob's own lips.'

Pierce stretches credibility even further when he assures us that Birmingham-bred rough-neck Phil Sampson was intended for a parson, but that 'he preferred thumping nobs to a cushion'! 'If so,' interjects the more down to earth *Pugilistica* in a passage which suggests Sampson could at least write his name, 'his acquirements in the *literae humaniores* did not say much for his college. Indeed, we have seen specimens of Philip's caligraphy which forbid such a tradition. What we know, however, is that young Phil was a button-maker in a Brummagem factory at fifteen!'

Each volume of *Boxiana* contains a welter of verbose chal-

The signature of John Gulley, ex-pugilist, parliamentarian and self-made millionaire, one of the few literate and financially successful men produced by the prize-ring.

lenges and counter-challenges, purporting to be from the leading boxers of the day, who, even if they could have written at all, were hardly likely to have used such absurdly over-blown language. Illiterate ex-slave Tom Molineaux is supposed to have penned the following example, following his initial defeat by Cribb:

> To Mr. Thomas Crib.
>
> *St. Martin's-street, Leicester-square,*
> *December* 21, 1810.
>
> Sir,
>
> My friends think, that had the weather on last Tuesday, the day upon which I contended with you, not been so unfavourable, I should have won the battle; I therefore challenge you to a second meeting, at any time within two months, for such a sum as those gentlemen, who place confidence in me, may be pleased to arrange.
>
> As it is possible that this letter may meet the public eye, I cannot omit the opportunity of expressing a confident hope, that the circumstances of my being of a different colour to that of the people amongst whom I have sought protection, will not in any way operate to my prejudice.
>
> I am, Sir,
> Your most obedient, humble Servant,
>
> T. MOLINEAUX.

By reprinting these wonderfully articulate but, alas ghosted inventions, Egan is continuing a literary tradition which goes back to the time of Mendoza and Humphries, when such correspondence supposedly between the rivals was first printed in the fashionable newspaper, the *World*. The genre, which in part gave rise to the myth that prize-fighters were all decent, polite, well-spoken fellows, was to continue beyond *Boxiana* until the final gasp of pugilism. It should be remembered that Egan and his contemporaries were writing to entertain as well as to inform an educated, if somewhat irresponsible public, who would probably have laughed heartily at such pretended erudition.

In addition to the verbiage contained in these challenges, Egan's own personal style is noted for the proliferation of dreadful puns, which, along with his use of sporting slang, become more and more extreme in each succeeding volume of *Boxiana*. Here the author introduces us to Jack Martin, a crack middleweight, who had worked in a bakery before turning to pugilism as a more profitable means of earning his 'bread':

> MARTIN has *hit* his way to NOTORIETY; and his *prowess*, before he entered the Prize Ring, was acknowledged by all the *crummy* and *crusty* customers, from one end to the other of the

Rolls Company. In short, he disposed of *batches* of the above heroes with so much ease and certainty, that his *title* of MASTER OF THE ROLLS, is now so established as to be entirely free from dispute.

Thereafter, throughout his long career, Martin was always 'The Master of the Rolls'. This continued a tradition in which every fighter of note had a *nom de guerre*, punning or otherwise, thrust upon him. Henry or Hen Pearce had been swiftly rechristened 'The Game Chicken', while Barney Aaron, an East End follower of Mendoza, became 'The Star of the East'. The practice of bestowing ring-names upon popular fighters has continued, with more or less absurd results, down to the present day.

It would have delighted Egan to know that he was also responsible for a pairing of names still associated with havoc a century and a half later. In 1821 between Volumes 2 and 3 of *Boxiana*, and numerous other minor publications, Egan, drawing on first-hand experience, produced a best-seller entitled: *Life in London or the Day and Night Scenes of Jerry Hawthorn, Esq. and his elegant friend, Corinthian Tom in their Rambles and Sprees through the Metropolis*. Best remembered today for the splendid Cruikshank illustrations, *Life in London* was, and still is, essential reading for anyone wishing to understand the pas-

A splendid illustration by the Cruikshank brothers, to Egan's Life in London. *Mortimers' 'Set-to' can be seen above the door.*

Drawn & Eng.ᵈ by I.R. & G. Cruikshank

ART OF SELF DEFENCE. *Tom and Jerry receiving Instructions from Mr. Jackson, at his Rooms, in Bond Street.*

Pub.ᵈ by Sherwood, Neely & Jones, Jan.ᵗ 1, 1821.

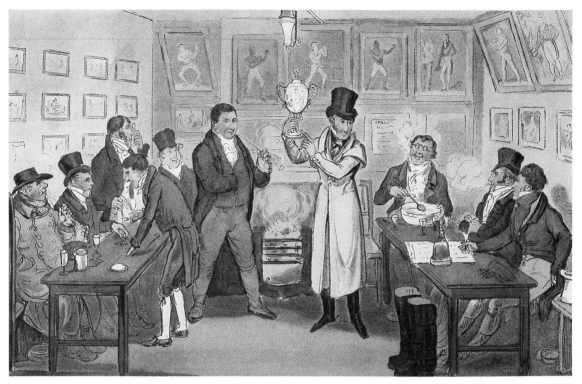

times and diversions of fashionable young Corinthians in the early part of the last century. The manners, dress and behaviour of Egan's heroes, Tom and Jerry, were much imitated by 'disorderly gentlemen' of the time, and the names became synonymous with the alcoholic excesses so common in the Regency period and during the reign of King George IV. A 'Tom and Jerryism' was the expression still in use in the latter part of the nineteenth century to describe such activities as knocking off policemen's helmets, or stealing and driving away hansom cabs, complete with passengers. The name was then given to a highly potent cocktail much loved by fast young men, which later became a favourite tipple in the United States, where Tom and Jerry were eventually re-born as the riotous cat and mouse characters so popular today.

Life in London was followed within two years by Egan's edition of *Grose's Classical Dictionary of the Vulgar Tongue, with the addition of Numerous Slang Phrases*, a publication indispensible to anybody wishing to understand the 'flash patter' with which the works of our author are inundated. Egan, who can be said to have been addicted to slang, recorded current words and phrases assiduously, adding them to the already considerable collection assembled by Francis Grose in the previous century, but we are directly indebted to the imagination of the author of *Boxiana* for quite a number of the pugilistic terms to be found in the *Dictionary*. When in his fight reports Egan had been stumped for the appropriate expression, he quite often,

'Cribb's parlour: Tom introducing Jerry and Logic to the Champion of England'. A hand-coloured aquatint engraving by George and Robert Cruikshank for Egan's Life in London.

'King Dick' Curtis dressed in the acme of fashion, a drawing by George Sharples, engraved for the Boxiana *of 1828, the year in which this brilliant lightweight lost his unbeaten record to Jack Perkins, 'The Oxford Pet'.*

in the best tradition of vernacular English, simply invented it and in this way the peculiar language of pugilism evolved. Whereas the current technical term 'the mark', denoting solar plexus, derives from 'Broughton's mark' as recorded by Captain Godfrey, and 'bread basket' the slang equivalent of 'the mark' also pre-dates Egan by fifty years, many of the bellicose expressions still in use today, such as 'mill' for fight or 'bunch of fives' meaning fist, can be traced directly back to the pages of *Boxiana*.

On the subject of Egan's prolific and ever-increasing use of slang, it is interesting to compare one of his later fight descriptions with the comparatively sober Cribb *v.* Molineaux report of 1811. Here we see a mature author in full flight. The occasion is the meeting in 1828 between the hitherto unbeaten Dick Curtis, 'The Pet of the Fancy', and the far heavier 'Oxford Pet', Jack Perkins, as recorded in *Pierce Egan's Book of Sports and Mirror of Life*. Five minutes of the first round had been spent in feinting and manoeuvring for an opening, with neither boxer attempting a blow:

> This most certainly, was a *new feature* in the battles of Curtis; and extorted from the backers of the Pet that Perkins was '*a troublesome customer*!' 'Go to work,' was the cry. Dick at length placed a slight facer; and in the exchange of hits, in a rally, he napt a rum one between the *chaffer* and the *sneezer*, which Spring [the second of Perkins] called out, 'First blood! and we shall win it!' This was another *new feature*! The Pet was on the alert, and planted a heavy blow on Perkins's *domino* box!

However Curtis was gradually worn down by superior weight until in the eighth round:

> Both men rallied like nothing else but *out-of-outers*; and lots of *claret* trickled down their faces. The blows were hard and fast, and a lunging one from Perkins, *floored* the PET like a SHOT! *The row was immense*; the *Classical Gents were almost out of their senses with joy at this sudden slice of luck.* 'Perkins for ever! Perkins for 1000l.' THE LONDONERS WERE PANIC STRUCK – *The bolting of the Great Stakeholder near the Blunt Magazine, could not be worse to their feelings*; – the latter hit was a *Rowland* for an Oliver – they were all reduced to DUMMIES in the twinkling of an eye – silence was the order of the day – their *choppers* as long as Patterson's Road Book, and blue, green, yellow, and all manner of colours *summut* like the incantation scene in *Der Frieschulz*.

The brave but overmatched Curtis was finally knocked out of time in the eleventh round and had to be carried unconscious from the ring, while the victor walked around with his friends:

His *nob* was not much *damaged*, excepting a cut over the left eye; his mug was *puffed* a little, but his *Grub Warehouse*, we think, must have been very tender, from the numerous *podgers* DICK planted upon it.

After the final volume of *Boxiana* had appeared in 1829, Egan's interest in the doings of the prize-ring began, along with that of society in general, to wane. Although, *Pierce Egan's Book of Sports and Mirror of Life*, published three years later, still contained vigorous first-hand descriptions of several major fights, the emphasis had shifted towards horse racing and other supposedly more respectable field sports.

In the 1840s, towards the end of his long life, Egan began to travel the country, delivering a series of lectures which extolled 'the Art of Self-Defence'. These talks were largely composed of an old man's reminiscences of the great days of pugilism, and formed the basis of Egan's final publication *Every Gentleman's Manual: A lecture on the Art of Self-Defence*, which appeared in 1845. It is fitting that Egan's last publication should, like his first of over thirty years earlier, deal exclusively with pugilism.

Friend and confidant of both bruisers and their backers, composer and singer of dozens of popular 'chaunts', referee and stakeholder at hundreds of prize-fights, chronicler of literally thousands of claret-soaked, bare-knuckle rounds, Egan's racy style was to serve as a model of fight reportage throughout pugilism's history. In fact, he can almost be said to have invented sporting journalism. He is the single most important figure in the recording of the ring's early history and remains perhaps the greatest of boxing reporters.

Back in 1822, and within a year of Egan's success with *Life in London*, there had appeared the first number of a general sporting, but mainly pugilistic, Sunday newspaper which appropriated *Life in London* as its title. The editor of the new publication even went so far as to call himself 'Bob Logic', the name earlier bestowed by Egan upon the alcoholic Oxonian companion of Tom and Jerry.

The paper was soon taken over by Robert Bell, who for some years previously had employed Egan on a regular basis to write fight reports for his *Weekly Dispatch*. The new publication, soon to be re-named *Bell's Life in London*, later absorbed the *Weekly Dispatch*, but not before the publishers had, for reasons no longer clear, added injury to insult by entirely severing connections with Egan. Not so easily beaten, Egan began to write and publish his own Sunday newspaper: *Pierce Egan's Life in London and Sporting Guide*. This competitor at first sold well, the fame of the author of *Boxiana* no doubt acting as a 'draw', but in less than four years Egan was forced to sell out, and in 1827 his short-lived publication was incorporated into *Bell's Life*, which, with an average circulation of between

The stiffly drawn figure of cockney pug 'Deaf' Burke stands full square in an idyllic English landscape. This hand-coloured aquatint by Charles Hunt, from a painting by Henry Meyer, was published on 24 February 1839, just twelve days after the 'Invincible' Burke had butted 'Bendigo' and thereby lost his claim to the championship.

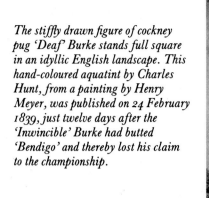

The Fives Court in London's St Martin's Lane, was the favourite meeting place of the 'Fancy'. This 1821 aquatint by Charles Turner after T. Blake, represents Randall sparring with Ned Turner, while in the foreground may be recognised every well-known prize-fighter of the time.
REPRODUCED BY COURTESY OF T. TULLEY.

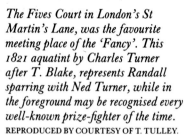

Pb March 1.. 1812 .. R. Rowlandson N° James Street
adelphi

Rowlandson 1812

DESCRIPTION OF A BOXING MATCH. June 9th 1812

Battle between Ward and Quirk for 100 Guineas aside — Remarks, A more determined and spirited contest than this
has seldom been witnessed, the first twelve Rounds were exceedingly hard fought without the slightest attempt to shift on either side,
Ward had a decided advantage over his opponent in the science of the art of boxing, and he shewed himself a much better hitter than
Quirk. The loss of the contest might in a great measure be attributed to his gaity for he was full of fight until his
strength failed him, which with an accidental hit deprived him altogether of defending himself, the beating he received
was nothing in comparison to what he had given, for his opponents head was swelled hideously, and his eyes were invisible.

A typically chaotic scene by Thomas Rowlandson, depicting the Ward versus Quirk contest of 1806. Both this engraving, published six years after the event, and the eye-witness drawing on which it was based, forcefully convey the ring-side atmosphere, rather than the more usual formality of the pugilistic set-piece.

twenty-five and thirty thousand copies each Sunday, was to remain the foremost sporting journal throughout the era of pugilism, and is, in succession to *Boxiana*, our primary source of prize-ring history.

Following Egan's departure from *Bell's Life*, the proprietors appointed Vincent George Dowling as editor. Dowling was, like Egan, a Londoner of Irish descent, but from a completely different social background. Vincent's father had been a bookseller who was also connected in some way with *The Times*. His younger brother, James, became a barrister and was knighted for his services as Chief Justice of New South Wales, while his youngest brother, Alfred, was also called to the Bar and achieved some fame as a law reporter. Despite being every inch a gentleman and a scholar, and claiming with some justification to have been the author of a plan upon which Sir Robert Peel's police force was organised, Vincent, with his predilection for prize-fighting, appears to have been the black sheep of the family.

Along with his brothers, Dowling received a good formal education, and by his late teens had become a regular contributor to various prestigious national newspapers, including *The Observer*. In this capacity he led an exciting life; for instance when the Prime Minister, Spencer Percival, was assassinated in the lobby of the House of Commons in 1812, young Dowling had been among the first to seize and disarm the murderer. He sometimes went to extraordinary lengths to obtain a scoop for his newspaper, as when in 1820 he sailed to France and returned in an open rowing boat on a stormy night to be the first with the news that Queen Caroline was about to embark for England to rejoin and embarrass her estranged husband who had just succeeded to the throne as King George the Fourth.

Two years earlier Dowling had reported his first prize-fight. Now, as editor of *Bell's Life*, he was to remain among pugilism's staunchest supporters during the last great years and throughout the ring's decline in the 1830s and 1840s. Well connected, scrupulously honest and possessed of a charming manner, Dowling was constantly named as stakeholder and referee at important fights. Often to be seen at ringside in company with Egan, the two men remained on the best of terms, and despite any professional jealousy which might have existed, Egan was to describe his rival as 'a most excellent companion; cheerful, witty, and satirical at all times, but, in the latter display of his talents, the *feather* appears more than the razor – he tickles his adversaries, rather than wounds their feelings.' Upon the death of Egan in 1849, Dowling reciprocated by inserting a glowing obituary in *Bell's Life*. Having declared 'The editor of *Boxiana*, the class-book of the fistic art . . . an historian in his way as great Plutarch,' he goes on to praise his friend in a style which consciously owes much to the subject of his eulogy. Dowling's fight reporting, whilst exploiting the advantage of a good education, had often followed in the wake of Egan's racy, rollicking, slangy style, and in his final tribute he acknowledged a great debt of gratitude.

Here, the editor of *Bell's Life* describes Bill Perry, 'The Tipton Slasher', immediately prior to that fighter's speedy demolition in 1846 of fellow Black-Country pug, Tass Parker. Having dealt enthusiastically with the graceful and attractive stance of Parker, which was coupled with a smiling and confident countenance, he then switches attention to the redoubtable Tiptonian:

> His massive and ungainly antagonist offered a striking contrast; brown, burly, and, as Paddy would say, 'big for his size,' he grinned grotesquely at his slighter rival, nor was the oddity of his mirthful mug by any means lessened by the fact of his front railings having been displaced in by-gone battles. He, too, was hard, and had evidently been brought by severe training into as good condition as we have ever seen him on former occasions. From the waist to the shoulders he was a model for a gladiator, but we doubt if the artist or the sculptor would feel inclined to copy his capital or his pedestals, inasmuch as the first is, despite a comic expression of good humour, as odd a conglomeration of features as Gillray or Cruickshank would desire to pencil; while the latter more resembles the letter K than the parallel supports which society has agreed to term symmetrical. His weight was 13st. 4lbs.; his age 27, having been born in 1819, although the displacement of his grinders gave him a more antique aspect.

Vincent George Dowling, for thirty years the editor of Bell's Life. *This wood-engraving of a bust of Timothy Butler accompanied Dowling's obituary in* The Illustrated London News.

REPRODUCED BY COURTESY OF
THE ILLUSTRATED LONDON NEWS.

Having disposed of Parker in twenty-seven minutes, 'The Slasher' later faced Tom Paddock, 'The Redditch needle-pointer', for the Championship of England. Dowling's son Frank was at hand and on this occasion almost out-Egan's both his father and Egan with surreal terminology. In the train down to the battlefield we are informed that: 'The men were in separate carriages, and there was a wide contrast in their bearing, Paddock being all mercurial and double jolly, and the Slasher as solid and steady as Doctor Wiseman on a fast day.' During the fight itself Paddock had all the worst of it: in addition to receiving 'a nasty "polthogue" on the nob' he 'jumped up like a parched pea'. By the 27th round it was all over bar the shouting:

> The odds were the Great Glass-case of '51 against a shirt-stitchers thimble. The Tipton gave Mister Paddock a pelt on the head and began punching at him among the bottles and traps at the corner stake. Paddock dropped, and the Tipton, fearing to give a charge away, was about to

return to his own corner, as he had several times done, when up jumped the Redditch man, and rushing at the Slasher, lent him such a dig just at the back of the left ear, with his right, that down tumbled Tipton, half with astonishment, half with the blow, and, as Paddy would say, 'the third half of him fell just because it was not used to stand up.' A more palpable foul was never seen.

Tom Paddock unfortunately made something of a habit of fouling his opponents: only six months before losing to 'The Tipton' he had given away another chance of the championship when, exasperated by the shifty tactics of Bendigo, he had twice struck that worthy while the latter was down. Having lost the fight by this means, he then compounded his crime by flooring his erstwhile opponent in front of the referee, who on this occasion was Vincent Dowling himself. In the by now customary riot which followed, some of Paddock's supporters chose to express their displeasure with an attack on the officials, and the sixty-five-year-old Dowling was struck on the back of the head with a bludgeon, a blow which momentarily paralysed him. The timely intervention of Tom Spring saved him from further harm, but the damage was done; it appears likely that the once robust reporter never fully recovered from the effects of the injury, and paralysis was stated as one of the causes of his death, which occured two years later.

In 1851, during Dowling's final illness, the editorship of *Bell's Life* was taken over by his son, Frank, who also continued the publication of *Fistiana*, which had been founded by his father in 1840 and was boxing's first annual record book. The younger Dowling now endeavoured to continue the family tradition of financial and moral support for the beleaguered prize-ring, which, like his father, he regarded as 'a means of maintaining a manly love of fair play'.

Frank, who, following in his uncle's footsteps, had been called to the Bar in 1847, inherited his father's tastes, together with his charm and urbanity. As we have seen he also inherited his style of editorship; the pages of *Bell's Life* continued to drip with claret: ogles shew mouses and eventually shut up shop, ivories are rattled, corks are drawn, and the best double-distilled is produced in torrents, especially when snouts are jobbed. At the same time rib-benders, pile-drivers and smacks on the gob continue to jostle with paragraphs of surprising erudition in a manner which cannot have failed to please even the more crusty of Oxford and Cambridge subscribers.

It was Dowling who organised the great international prize-fight between Sayers and Heenan in 1860, at which he acted as referee and was instrumental in declaring the match a draw. Afterwards he set up the subscription fund which provided a silver championship belt for each man, in addition to a collection for the retiring Tom Sayers, which amounted to an astonishing £3,000!

Unfortunately, Frank Dowling was, like his hero Tom Sayers, consumptive, and he died at an early age in 1867. He was one of the last gentleman supporters of pugilism, and without his steadying influence and unflagging efforts in match-making the ailing prize-ring's days were numbered. True, *Bell's Life* struggled on for another twenty years, with less and less boxing to report, but its time, like that of pugilism itself, was past. The ring had in reality died with Dowling.

As an annual distillation of *Bell's Life*, the pocket volume *Fistiana* had continued to chronicle the current doings of the prize-ring, reaching its twenty-fourth and final edition in 1864, but nothing approaching a complete history of pugilism had been attempted since the first volume of *Boxiana*, more than half a century earlier.

The challenge of collecting and collating the vast amount of material contained in the writings of Egan, the Dowlings and a host of lesser scribes, was taken up during the final years of *Bell's Life* by Henry Downes Miles. Now in his seventies, Miles was eminently qualified for such an undertaking, having written a *Handbook of Boxing and Training for Athletic Sports* as early as 1838, and a *Life of Tom Sayers*, under the *nom de plume* of *Philopugilis*, in 1864. Between these two dates Miles had edited various sporting magazines, and worked for many years as a reporter on both *Bell's Life* and the pugilistically inclined *Morning Advertiser*.

In 1863 Miles finally published the fruits of his painstaking research under the title of: *Pugilistica – One Hundred and Forty Years of British Boxing*. Up-dated and reissued in 1880, this three volume *magnum opus* uses *Boxiana* as a model whilst continually denigrating the scholarship of the author, whom it refers to ironically as 'the historian'. Whether or not this somewhat scathing attitude mars an otherwise excellent publication is a matter of opinion, but it must be admitted that the occasional censure of Egan's more extreme flights of fancy, especially concerning the early careers of his favourites, does go some way towards setting the record straight, whilst in no way detracting from the originality of the earlier author's unique style.

Pugilistica, although far more prosaic than either Egan or the Dowlings, is scrupulously accurate and contains a vast amount of observation, both of pugilism and of the social customs and manners of the times. Although Miles' memory did not quite stretch back to the ring's great days in the twenties, he did remember the likes of Cribb and Spring during their retirement and included within his text are some excellent personal anecdotes, as for instance the touching death-bed interview with old Jem Burn, whose speech and

Frank Dowling, the editor of Bell's Life, *acted as referee for the great fight of 1860. He is pictured here at the Farnborough ringside, seated on the ground between ex-champion Ben Caunt and a gentleman amateur.*
REPRODUCED BY COURTESY OF T. TULLEY.

A Punch *cartoon, in which 'Charles reads from* Bell's Life, *eloquently conveys the ambiguous attitude of the respectable Victorian middle-class to the international contest of 1860.* Punch *devoted no less than ten cartoons and a full-page poem to the fight.*

REPRODUCED BY COURTESY OF *PUNCH*.

SERIOUS GOVERNOR. "*I am surprised, Charles, that you can take any interest in these repulsive details—how many Rounds (I believe you term them) do you say these ruffians fought? Um, disgraceful! the Legislature ought to interfere, and——it appears then that this Benicia Man did not gain the—hem—best of it. I'll take the paper when you have done with it, Charles.*"

opinions are recorded in a jargon worthy of Captain Cuttle:

> For several years, as Jem grew in years and in portliness, and, though not a hard drinker, fully enjoyed the good things of this life, he was subject to intermittent attacks of gout, which, towards 1862, assailed him with increasing frequency, yet failing, when they gave him even a short truce, to subdue his natural fun and frolic. It was during one of unusual severity that we looked in to inquire after Jem's health, and his pleasant daughter having taken up our name, the bedridden boxer desired us to be 'shown up'. We expressed our sympathy, regarding at the same time with some curiosity a contrivance suspended from the curtain-rods of the four-poster in which Jem was recumbent.
>
> 'Ha! old fellow,' said the merry Yorkshireman [Miles, having constantly chastised Egan for his Hibernisation of the leading fighters, himself continues the time-honoured tradition of supposing everyone born north of Watford to be

a Yorkshireman: Burn, in fact, hailed from Darlington, County Durham] 'you're wanting to spell out the meaning of that. I'll tell you, if this blessed crab that's just now got me in *toe* don't give his claw an extra squeeze. If he does, why, I'll strike, and he shall *tow* me into port at once.'

'No, Jem, it's not come to that yet.'

'But it very soon must, if it don't stalk. See here,' said he, pointing to a strong cord stretched from the top rail across the bed, from which another cord was suspended midway, and made fast to the handle of an old-fashioned corkscrew. 'If it warn't for this tackle I'd get no sleep night nor day. Inside the bedclothes I've got a bung – good idea for a licensed victualler – into that I screws the corkscrew through the bedclothes, which I then raise tent-fashion by this hal'yard, and that I make fast down here to the bed-post. There's a wrinkle for you, Miles's Boy; but I hope you'll never want it for yourself.' Poor Jem we never saw again. His arch-enemy ascended to his portly stomach, and on the morning of the 29th May Jem slept with his forefathers.

In addition to reprinting the reports of *Bell's Life* et al, many of the fights are described with first-hand zest, but unfortunately after about 1835 *Pugilistica* deals only with the exploits of the champions and their opponents, space not permitting any record of the contests engaged in by the smaller men. Miles, probably the last of a generation who remembered pugilism in full swing, had intended to publish the lives and careers of lightweights such as Owen Swift, Johnny Walker and Johnny Broom, and he might have told us much more about the Dowlings and Egan, but he was prevented, to the irrevocable loss of the modern reader, by the advancing years.

At the beginning of the twentieth century there appeared Fred Henning's *Fights for the Championship*, published by the Licensed Victuallers Association. Aimed, one presumes, at Edwardian publicans, many of whom were ex-boxers, this close-set and appallingly illustrated production is very much a distillation of *Pugilistica*, with additional anecdotes and information about the later champions. If Henning's work lacks the verve and first-hand excitement of the earlier eye-witness accounts, it was at least a fairly reliable substitute for the by now out of print volumes of Egan and Miles.

By the time that *Pugilistica* was finally reprinted in 1906, only old Jem Mace and a handful of other septuagenarians were still alive who could remember anything of the English prize-ring, or refute some of the more blatant misrepresentations already becoming popular. The 'ripping yarn' type of literature masquerading as history, with which pugilism has since been dogged, had already received the following summary admonition from Miles:

Foremost of these is a weekly newspaper professing to be the Argus of the Turf, and the Titan of Tipsters. The 'Famous Old Fights' appearing in its columns are pure fiction, grafted on well-known names, dates, and anecdotes procurable from standard works of reference; the details of incidents, of rounds &c., &c., being the emanation of the lively imagination of the newswriter, who, to our knowledge, and from the innumerable instances in his blundering romance, is utterly ignorant and innocent of any acquaintance with the Ring, its professors, or the scenes he so inventively describes.

John L. Sullivan tries a left to the head of England's Charlie Mitchell during their drawn battle of 1888, which took place at Chantilly, France. This contest, at least, was described fairly accurately, unlike many of less recent date, within the pages of Famous Fights.

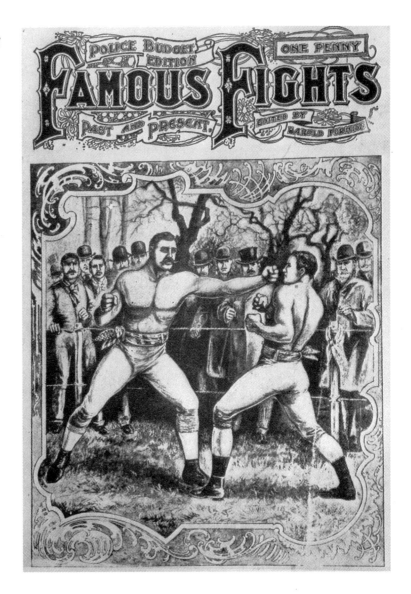

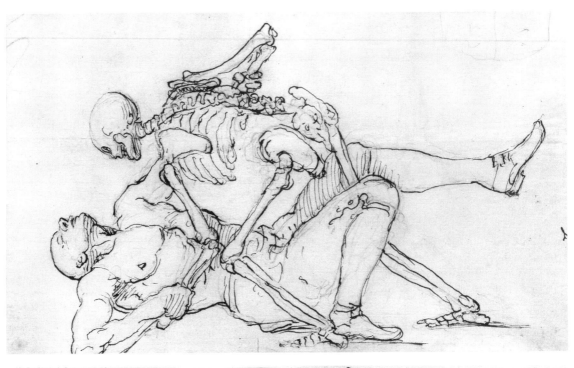

CHAPTER 7

TOMBS AND *EPITAPHS*

Yet bravely I'll dispute the prize,
nor yield, though out of breath,
'Tis not a fall – I yet shall rise,
And conquer even Death!

'BIG BEN' BRAIN'S EPITAPH, 1794

When George Taylor died a few months after a fight in 1758, his tombstone was designed by no less an artist than William Hogarth. This memorial, if ever produced, has long since disappeared, but the existing cartoon shows the pugilist, appropriately dressed for the prize-ring, receiving his own favourite throw, a cross-buttock, from Death himself. In the companion scene, Taylor, now wearing a classical loincloth, triumphs in turn over his skeletal adversary.

REPRODUCED BY COURTESY OF YALE CENTRE FOR BRITISH ART, PAUL MELLON COLLECTION.

Throughout prize-ring history, the comparatively small proportion of fighters who died as a direct result of their profession were quietly buried in unmarked graves after the briefest of funeral services. Rather more time and energy was spent evading the authorities' efforts to bring to book the surviving boxer, along with seconds, bottleholders, backers, umpires and other accessories.

A notable exception was made in the case of George Earl, who died after fighting with game and clever Tom Tyne in front of the grandstand on Brighton racecourse. The Prince of Wales and a large party from the Pavilion were among the spectators. A contemporary report states that HRH 'greatly to his honour immediately settled an annuity on the wife and family of Earl, and took the determination never to be present at another pugilistic contest'. The author of *Pugilistica* rather scornfully adds, 'We hope the first promise was kept better than the second.'

The fact that this early ring fatality was reported at all was due solely to the scandal caused by the presence of royalty. Deaths which had occurred in previous fights had gone largely unnoticed by a press unconcerned with the fate of the common man, and poor Earl was to achieve undying fame from a combination of royal patronage and the immortal lines said to have been engraved upon his tombstone:

George Earl, Boxer, 6 August 1788, Gave In.

Reports of ring deaths continued intermittently into the nineteenth century and then suddenly increased to a marked degree in the 1830s. A probable reason for this, leaving aside more humane and vigilant newspaper coverage, was the withdrawal from pugilism at this period of many of the aristocratic backers to whom loss of stake-money was relatively unimportant. Their replacement by speculators who

137

needed to win at any cost exposed a flaw of paramount importance in Broughton's Rules which state that at the beginning of a round 'each second is to *bring* his man' to the centre of the ring. In practice, a strong second in danger of losing his money was less inclined to throw in the sponge and could bring a half dead man up to scratch for 'just one more round'. Consequently, fights became more protracted.

The fatal championship fight of 1833 in which Deaf Burke beat Simon Byrne after a gruelling three hours and sixteen minutes, combined with the deaths of Anthony Noon in 1834 and 'Brighton Bill' Phelps in 1838, both in fights with Owen Swift, served to draw the attention of several financially disinterested gentlemen to the fact that times had changed and the rules needed to change with them. The ninth of the 29 rules which in 1838 replaced the mere seven of Broughton, clearly states 'that on the expiration of thirty seconds the umpire shall cry "Time", upon which each man shall rise from the knee of his bottleholder and walk to his own side of the scratch *unaided*. The seconds and bottleholders remaining at their corner.'

Although ring deaths do not cease thereafter, they do at least become less frequent.

Before the emergence of the Welfare State, premature death had been accepted as the usual fate of the masses, and the outwardly robust pugilist was no exception. The list of fighters who died young outside the ring reads like a pugilistic roll of honour: Jem Belcher, Hen Pearce, Jack Randall, Dan Donnelly, Josh Hudson, Young Dutch Sam and Tom Sayers were all dead before the age of forty. Apart from the practice of professional fighting, the common link between the above pugilists is that they all died while plying the trade of licensed victualler.

During the era of pugilism, drinking reached epidemic proportions throughout all classes of English society, and at the lower end of the scale beer houses and gin palaces were at the height of their popularity. Behind the bar of these establishments would more often than not be found a bruiser or ex-bruiser, and the pugilist came to be regarded as merely 'a publican in pupa stage'.

In *Dombey and Son*, Dickens' drunken pug, known as The Game Chicken, 'who was always to be heard of at the bar of The Black Badger . . . dipped his beak into a tankard' a little too often and, having duly been beaten by The Larky Boy, was forced to consider alternative employment. He therefore resolved not to leave his patron 'for any less consideration than the goodwill and fixtures of a public house . . . being ambitious to go into that line and drink himself to death as soon as possible.' The truth was, unfortunately, often not far removed from this caricature.

The 'Nonpareil', Jack Randall, can be taken as a fair

representative of the hard-drinking fraternity. Jack was for a few years landlord of the 'Hole in the Wall', a well-known sporting house in Chancery Lane, where eventually 'his constitution – he was a persistent drinker of ardent spirits – gave way under the irregularities of a licensed victualler's life; Jack never possessed the moral courage to say "No" to a drop with every customer who proposed to "wet an eye", and but rarely with those who suggested to "wet the other". He was a martyr to gout, complicated by a disorganisation of the liver and a fatty degeneration of the heart. These disorders prostrated him, and finally carried him off at the early age of 34 years.'

In the absence of any detailed medical evidence, we may surmise that the common cause of premature death among prize-fighters were injuries sustained in the ring, and the appalling regime of reducing and training undergone before each fight, combined with the inability or unwillingness of many fighters to refuse drinks from the numerous admirers who flocked to the various boxing pubs. Drunk rather than punch-drunk would seem to be the description most likely to apply to many pugilists who died in their prime.

In contrast to the norm, Jack Broughton, 'The Father of Boxing', survived to a very advanced age, as can be gathered from the epitaph reputedly carved on the old fighter's tombstone in his local church of St Mary-at-Lambeth:

> Hic Jacet Iohannes Broughton
> Pugil aevi svi praestantissimus
> Obit Die Octavo Ianvarii
> Anno Salvtis 1789
> Ætatis svae 85.

> Here lies John Broughton
> The foremost boxer of the age
> Who died the eighth of January
> In the year of our salvation 1789
> In the 85th year of his age.

Although Broughton certainly seems to have been buried at St Mary's, his inscription, like that to George Earl, has unfortunately disappeared and beyond a reference in the *Dictionary of National Biography*, there is no evidence that it ever existed. The mystery is compounded by the fact that Westminster Abbey, just across the Thames from Lambeth, also claims his grave. There is a stone slab still to be seen in the cloisters, inscribed with the words:

> Mr John Broughton
> Died Janry 8th 1789
> Aged 86 years

Wherever his final resting place might be, Broughton is said to have died worth £7,000, but most of his immediate successors who survived both the rigours of the prize-ring and the adulations attendant upon victory died in abject poverty, were buried in unmarked graves and promptly forgotten.

But as the eighteenth century gave way to the nineteenth, with the ever-present threat of invasion from just across the English Channel, successful boxers, as a personification of British pluck and endurance, began to be revered as national heroes. A nation at war, or under the constant threat of war, requires heroes, and heroes have to be commemorated with monuments.

The earliest and grandest of the resulting memorials was raised above the grave in Brompton Cemetary of Byron's 'corporal pastor and master', John Jackson.

For a quarter of a century up until 1824, it had been a social requirement for young men of fashion to take boxing instruction from Mr Jackson in his rooms at Number 13 Old Bond Street. In fact, 'not to have taken lessons from Jackson was a reproach. To attempt a list of his pupils would be to copy one third of the then peerage.'

What Wellington had been to the army, so Jackson was to pugilism. He officiated as Master of Ceremonies, or 'Commander in Chief' at most of the important fights during the heyday of the prize-ring, and was reported to be on nodding terms with King George IV, at whose coronation he headed a corps of prize-fighters dressed as royal pages, possibly employed to keep the estranged Queen Caroline and her supporters out of Westminster Hall.

When he died in 1845 at the age of seventy-seven, Jackson's friends and former pupils did not forget him, and a subscription was raised by 'several noblemen and gentlemen, to record their admiration of one whose excellence of heart and incorruptible worth endeared him to all who knew him'.

The tomb, executed within two years by the fashionable sculptor Timothy Butler, is described as 'handsome' in the pages of *Pugilistica*, although 'hideous' had been the epithet bestowed by the *Builder* of 1872. The monument, perhaps rather more in accordance with today's taste than with the universal Gothic of our Victorian forebears, comprises a large plinth, one side of which bears a portrait and the other an eulogy of the departed hero. Above the plinth crouches a huge British lion, no doubt intended to reflect the noble qualities of the deceased. At one time a lifesize representation of Jackson as a nude gladiator stood in front, plunged in grief, with a strategically placed laurel wreath coyly clasped in his right hand. The present-day visitor will find the gladiator unfortunately replaced with a far less amusing urn in memory of Jackson's niece, who had been the old champion's constant companion during his last years. The inscription, perhaps the best of its kind, remains unchanged:

> 'Stay, traveller,' the Roman records said,
> To mark the classic dust beneath it laid; –
> 'Stay, traveller,' this brief memorial cries,
> And read the record with attentive eyes.
> Hast thou a lion's heart, a giant's strength?
> Exult not, for these gifts must yield at length.
> Do health and symmetry adorn thy frame?
> The mouldering bones below possessed the same.
> Does love, does friendship every step attend?
> This man ne'er made a foe, ne'er lost a friend.
> But death too soon dissolves all human ties,
> And, his last combat o'er, here Jackson lies.

A few months after the unveiling of Jackson's monument, the death occurred of supreme national hero Tom Cribb; within a year between the Peninsular War victories of Corunna and Salamanca he had twice defeated black Tom Molyneaux, who to the xenophobic British populace represented that other enemy, the upstart American. At that time and right up to his death the name of Tom Cribb exuded the same sort of nationalist charisma as those of Nelson or Sir John Moore:

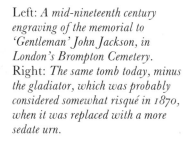

Left: *A mid-nineteenth century engraving of the memorial to 'Gentleman' John Jackson, in London's Brompton Cemetery.*
Right: *The same tomb today, minus the gladiator, which was probably considered somewhat risqué in 1870, when it was replaced with a more sedate urn.*

Since boxing is a manly game,
And Britons' recreation;
By boxing we will raise our fame,
'Bove any other nation.

If Boney doubt it let him come,
And try with Cribb a round;
And Cribb shall beat him like a drum,
And make his carcase sound.

In the spring of 1848, 'The last sad duty of consigning Tom's remains to their final resting place was performed in Woolwich churchyard, his ashes mingling with those of naval and military heroes honourably distinguished in their respective vocations.' A fitting mausoleum would have to be prepared!

Vincent Dowling, the editor of *Bell's Life*, together with some friends and admirers of the champion, including the now usual host of 'noblemen and gentlemen of the highest rank', resolved to erect a monument to Cribb's memory. By the beginning of 1851 *Bell's Life* could report that:

> Among the interesting incidents connected with the approaching . . . Great Exhibition, we have much pleasure in announcing the completion of the long promised monument to the memory of Tom Cribb, one of the most justly esteemed champions of the pugilistic school of England.
>
> As a professor of his art he was matchless, and as a demonstrator of fair play, in principle and in practice, he was never excelled. He had a still higher virtue, displayed in sustaining throughout his gallant career, independent of indomitable courage – a reputation for unimpeachable integrity and unquestionable humanity.
>
> Exception may be taken to the sphere in which those qualities were exhibited, but those acquainted with English feeling, English character and English habits must hold in estimation the memory of a man who, in his own person and by his own acts, impressed on thousands, we might say millions, those principles of fair play, combined with gallant bearing, which have been the distinguishing features of our countrymen, soldiers, sailors, or civilians, in whatever circumstances placed.

Dowling continues:

> We hardly doubt that this monument, from the moral it is calculated to enforce, will be without its beneficial effects on the minds of all those by whom it is seen, and we trust it may be gratifying to those strangers who on their visits to the Arsenal will have an opportunity of witnessing the veneration in which Englishmen hold the memory of those

who, although not 'licenced' warriors, are yet honest types of our national principles and character.

On the first of May 1854 the monument was placed in position. It had been executed by the same sculptor earlier responsible for John Jackson's tomb.

In Frank Dowling's opinion the artist had:

> . . . performed his task in a manner that must increase his reputation, and entitle him to a distinguished position in the profession of which he is so bright an ornament. The design is simple yet grand in its conception. It represents a British lion grieving over the ashes of a British hero; for, putting aside all prejudice, Cribb was a hero of whom his country might well be proud . . . We do not believe there is in existence a more beautiful specimen of animal sculpture, whether we regard the exquisite proportions of the figure, or the deep impression of sorrow expressed on the countenance.

It must be said that Dowling was a better judge of fighting-men than of sculpture: 'The paw of the lion, rests on an urn supposed to contain the ashes of the dead, over which is lightly thrown the belt which was presented to Cribb as Champion of England . . .'

There had been objections from some of the more sober-minded residents to the erection in their churchyard of such a monument to a common prize-fighter, and its final position there was due largely to the tolerance of the Reverend Greenlaw, who, it must be said, participated in the feelings of his parishioners to some degree. His objections were removed by the statement from Dowling that before work on the monument began, the design had been submitted to his predecessor, by whom it was heartily approved. The rector did, however, sustain an objection to the following inscription, which was omitted at his request:

> When some proud earl or rich patrician dies,
> Unmoved we mark the storied marble rise,
> Unmoved we read the praises blazoned forth,
> And doubt the meed if giv'n to wealth or worth;
> But truth shall guide this record, and proclaim
> Who raised himself without a crime to fame;
> Whose heart was tender as his arm was strong;
> Who still upheld the right, abhorred the wrong;
> Who stood unconquered champion in that field,
> Where hardy heroes nature's weapons wield –
> 'Twas poor Tom Cribb – beneath his ashes lie;
> Peace to his spirit's immortality!

In place of this were carved the simple words 'Respect the ashes of the dead', an inscription which Dowling had hoped would 'prevent those encroachments in which idle visitors to churchyards too often indulge'.

These anti-vandal sentiments of Dowling's were endorsed some years later by the addition of iron railings, which for a while lent the monument a rather pathetic zoo-like quality. The removal of these railings during the Second World War improved the appearance of the tomb, whilst unfortunately letting the vandals back in. Yet despite the unavoidable twentieth-century accompaniments of grafitti and litter, the great stone lion on its rock, carved from a twenty-ton block of Portland stone, still looks out across the Thames, as indestructable as honest Tom was once deemed to be.

Cribb's protegé and adopted 'boy', Tom Spring, had visited the old champion on his death-bed; Cribb had suddenly sat up and, punching the air, uttered his last words, 'The action's still there but the steam's gone.' Spring himself was dead long before his 'old dad's' monument had been placed in position.

Cribb's monument as it appears today, overlooking the Woolwich Ferry, from high up in the Thames-side town's churchyard.

SACRED
TO THE MEMORY OF
THOMAS WINTER SPRING
BORN AT FOWNHOPE
HEREFORDSHIRE
FEBRUARY 22ᴬᴰ 1795
AND DIED
AT THE CASTLE TAVERN
HOLBORN
AUGUST 20ᵀᴴ 1851.

The monument erected in Norwood Cemetery to the memory of Tom Spring has weathered badly and now bears little resemblance to the imposing stone obelisk illustrated in Pugilistica.

Spring, whose real name was Winter, had died, universally respected at his famous pub, The Castle Tavern in Holborn, when 'pale death struck him down somewhat suddenly, the blow being dealt through a heart disease of some years' standing'. His funeral took place with 'becoming solemnity on Sunday, 25 August 1851' at the newly established South Metropolitan Cemetery in semi-rural West Norwood. He lies buried beneath a once handsome classical Greek obelisk which displayed a portrait of the departed hero above a carving of a lion reposing with a lamb, an allusion to the placid character displayed by this skilful boxer when outside the ring.

Spring was eulogised by George Borrow as a:

> . . . true species of English stuff . . . sharp as Winter, kind as spring . . . Hail to thee, last of England's bruisers, after all the manly victories which thou has achieved – true English victories, unbought by yellow gold; need I recount them? nay, nay! they are already known to fame – sufficient to say that Bristol's Bull and Ireland's champion were vanquished by thee, and one mightier still, gold itself thou didst overcome; for gold itself strove in vain to deaden the power of thy arm; and thus thou didst proceed till men left off challenging thee, the unvanquishable, the incorruptable [etc., etc.].

It comes as a great relief to learn that Borrow was *not* employed to write Tom's epitaph, which happily confined itself to name, date and place of birth and death. 'Peace be to his manes! Few men who have led a public life have less reason to dread the last call of "Time", than Thomas Winter Spring.'

Sharp winters, aided by souvenir-hunters, have been less than kind to Tom's soft sandstone monument, which is now in a tragically neglected condition. The carved portrait has long since disappeared, the inscription is now illegible and the remainder sadly continues to deteriorate from year to year.

Spring was buried next to local boy Ned Neal, 'The Streatham Youth', victor in no less than thirteen prize-fights. Neal's career had closed 'as with so many others, in defeat. Yet he retired with his laurels unsullied, his character for courage and honesty unsmirched; and respected by all who knew him, he "shuffled off this mortal coil" at The Rose and Crown, Norwood, in November 1846, aged 41.'

Ned's grave is covered by a large inscribed rectangular slab, which, like the tomb of his more famous neighbour, is now in an advanced state of decay.

Despite Borrow's assertion, Spring was not the 'last of England's bruisers'. The final great national hero produced by the prize-ring was possibly the greatest. This was good-natured and popular Tom Sayers who in 1860 had held the comparatively huge American, John Heenan, to a draw at the end of that most famous of fights, an epic contest which, despite the stifling anti-pugilistic tenor of the age, was regarded by all classes as an event in which national prestige really was at stake.

Thackeray was to write:

> . . . If I were absolute king, I would send Tom Sayers to the mill for a month, and make him Sir Thomas on coming out. You are a naughty boy, Tom! but then, you know, we ought to love our brethren, though ever so naughty. We are moralists, and reprimand you; and you are hereby reprimanded accordingly. But in case England should ever have need of a few score thousand champions, who laugh at danger; who cope with giants; who, stricken to the ground, jump up and gaily rally, and fall, and rise again, and strike, and die rather than yield – in case the country should need such men, and you should know them, be pleased to send lists of the misguided persons to the principal police stations, where means may some day be found to utilize their wretched powers, and give their deplorable energies a right direction.

Revered before the fight, Sayers was now elevated to the pantheon, and the prize-ring achieved one last great surge of popularity, before sinking into disgrace and oblivion.

On 10 November 1865 *The Times*, that pillar of respectability, which five years earlier had devoted no less than half a page to the fight, carried the following announcement:

> The death was reported yesterday morning of Tom Sayers, the Ultimus Romanorum of the prize ring, . . . he died at 6 o'clock last evening at his residence in Camden-town from disease of the lungs, which for some time led his friends to anticipate a fatal result. He wanted a few months of being 40 years of age.

'The Polydeuces of our country' went to his early grave in Highgate cemetery amid scenes which eclipsed anything hitherto witnessed at a funeral. The route was crowded with an estimated 100,000 people, including reporters from some of the quality papers as well as the popular press. Over fifty carriages, many bearing heraldic devices, jostled with brewers' drays and coal carts to form the cortège. Publicans had respectfully lowered their blinds and hung out crêped banners, while a roaring trade was conducted in the retail of photographic portraits of the deceased.

Amidst an atmosphere resembling that of a public holiday, or for that matter a great prize-fight, the hearse moved slowly along followed by a mail phaeton in which seated alone was Tom's constant companion and chief mourner, the huge mastiff dog 'Lion', his collar swathed in black crêpe.

Among the spectators a ballad-singer chanted verses in praise of the departed champion; the words were set to a popular tune and many of the assembled crowd joined in the choruses. Behind the carriages came the 'slow eyed, great jawed multitude from the East, clattering over the gravel walks, trampling with their clinkered boots over delicate marble slabs, and playing leap-frog with every sepulchral monument of a convenient height that stood in their way'.

The police were at hand to curtail the worst of the sacrilege and malicious damage, but the swearing and shouting of lively obscenities continued as the pile of earth from the newly dug grave was commandeered as a sort of ringside seat by some of the East End fancy.

Tom's friend, the Reverend Litten, who had administered the Last Sacrament, now conducted the service and pronounced a short eulogy as Tom was lowered into the grave: 'He was a true friend to those who trusted him and a generous giver to those in need.'

Within a few days a subscription towards the erection of a colossal marble figure was announced on the front page of *The Times*, but this seems to have come to nothing, although a more modest monument was soon erected over the grave by

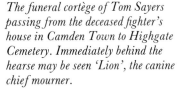

The funeral cortège of Tom Sayers passing from the deceased fighter's house in Camden Town to Highgate Cemetery. Immediately behind the hearse may be seen 'Lion', the canine chief mourner.

'A committee of friends, the admirers of true British courage'.

A quarter of a century later the writer Frederick Locker-Lampson, who as a young man had been present at the Sayers *v.* Heenan fight, happened to be in Highgate Cemetery and whilst looking at the monuments fell to talking with the custodian about the many distinguished people buried within its precincts:

'And then,' said he, 'we have another that used to be a deal talked about. You've heard, I suppose, of Tom Sayers, the fightin' man?' I had heard of Tom, and before I left the ground I found my way to his last resting place. It was not difficult to identify; for, although the inscription was almost effaced by time and weather, and the imagery was fast mouldering away, the grave was recognisable by a rather coarsely chiselled bas-relief which claimed to be the portrait of Tom himself, and by the sculptured effigy of his favourite mastiff, Lion. I should have liked there and then, to have sent for a monumental sculptor and had the inscription recut: but the custodian told me this was impossible. Litigation as to the possession of the grave was in progress,

Tom Sayers' constant companion, 'Lion' the mastif, lends an air of repose to his master's grave in Highgate 'old' Cemetery. In reality the animal became Lot 103 in a sale of the late champion's effects, and was sold to a north London publican for the staggering sum of thirty guineas.

and while that went on the stones could not be interfered with. In fact, a battle-royal was at that very moment raging over Fighting Tom's remains.

Possession of the grave was finally gained by Tom's son and namesake in 1891. The inscription and portrait were re-cut and 'Lion', the champion's chief mourner, still sits guarding his master. 'Alas, poor Tom!' mused Locker-Lampson. 'Like most of his calling he died a young man.'

Premature death of a more violent and sudden nature had been the fate of Tom Hickman, the hard-hitting, hard-drinking 'Gas Light Man'. In December 1822, having witnessed a fight near St Alban's, Hickman and a companion were driving back to London in a hired chaise. Both had been drinking heavily, even though Jack Randall later testified to the contrary.

It was dusk as they crossed Finchley Common and Hickman tried to overtake a wagon on the near side of the road. What followed reads like a chapter from one of the Gothic horror stories of the period: 'Whether from unskilful driving, the darkness of the night or some other cause[!], in clearing the wagon the chaise was overturned, and dreadful to relate, both were precipitated under the wheels, which went over their heads. Hickman was killed instantaneously, his brains were scattered on the road, and his head nearly crushed to atoms.'

His body, which was said to possess great anatomical beauty, remained unscathed and it was rumoured that the surgeons from Bart's Hospital, adjacent to Hickman's London pub, required the fresh corpse 'to make experiments on'. Accordingly his friends kept it eight days to disappoint them, and even when 'a whole peck of lime had been put into the coffin, right over the chest', it was still considered necessary to bury it in a grave eighteen feet deep to escape the attentions of the 'Resurrection men', upon whose nocturnal trade medical science was to remain dependent until the passing of the Anatomy Act of 1832.

The funeral affords a good example of the *esprit de corps* which then existed among fighting men, and of the esteem in which they were held by the general public. The list of mourners is like a directory of the Regency prize-ring:

On Thursday, December 19, a vast concourse of people assembled in Aldersgate Street and Jewin Street to witness the funeral of Hickman. At twelve o'clock the funeral procession commenced from the Adam and Eve, in Jewin Street, the house of Hickman ... The pall was supported by Josh Hudson and Shelton, Tom Belcher and Harmer, and Randall and Turner. The father of Gas, his brother, and some other relatives were the principal mourners. The procession was filled up by . . . Tom Owen, Scroggins, Parish, Oliver, Jem Burn, Purcell, Powell, Bill Davies, Baxter and Pierce Egan. The plate on the coffin stated Hickman to be in his twenty-seventh year. He was buried in the churchyard in Little Britain. On the ground were Bittoon, Bill Eales, Jack Carter, George Head, etc . . . The crowd in the streets was immense.

Hickman's widow and infant children were later given a tumultuous benefit at the Fives Court at which most of the leading pugilists of the day exhibited their skills. The door money amounted to the then not inconsiderable sum of £136.13s.6d. Not content with this, the pugilists took turns for several weeks in running the bar of the Adam and Eve and their efforts were 'crowned with success'. So it is to be hoped that Mrs Hickman at least gained some material comfort from the untimely death of her volatile and violent husband:

> Farewell to thee, Gasman! it grieves me to learn
> That, unknown and obscure, you took leave of Life's spark,
> That the miller, who ne'er from a foeman would turn,
> Had his Life's gas extinguished one night in the dark.

Macabre events, tinged with an element of black comedy, surround the death, burial and alleged resurrection of Hickman's contemporary, 'Sir' Daniel Donnelly.

Donnelly was an Irishman *par excellence*, 'a broth of a bhoy', strongly addicted to wine, women and song. His excesses in the first and second of these fields of activity finally caught up with him at his pub in Dublin:

Tom Hickman 'The Gasman', anti-hero and drunken driver.

> . . . on the 18th of February 1820, in consequence of having drunk a draught of cold water when in a state of perspiration, after an active game of fives. He was in the 34th year of his age. It is said, that his blood was overheated, from the great quantity of whisky punch, that Dan had taken on the preceding evening, to show some of his companions the insensible effects spirituous liquors had upon his constitution. But alas! Dan's judgement proved erroneous upon this suit.

After nine days, during which time, the customary celebrations occurred, and following a funeral attended by the usual vast mob, some of whom vied for the honour of drawing the hearse in place of horses, Dan's body was borne in triumph to the graveyard at Kilmainham, appropriately named Bully's Acre, and there laid to rest. But for how long?

A few days later the following letter appeared in the *Dublin Evening Post*:

Sir – Having attended the remains of the victorious DONN-ELLY to his last home, on Sunday, a curiosity of again beholding his grave, induced me, on passing that way this evening, to turn into the ground, accompanied by two friends: on coming to the Hero's grave, what was our surprise, to behold the clay thrown up, the coffin lid broken, and the body gone; – it immediately occurred to us, that the Resurrectionists, of York-street, had paid him a visit – we passed through Kilmainham, and were informed there, that during the last two nights a few admirers of his art, had been there to protect him, but their naturally jovial disposition, and the severity of the weather, prompted them to make too frequent libations on the tomb of the departed Champion, and disabled them from perceiving or opposing those riflers of the House of Death. I communicate this intelligence through an idea that the public may be gratified in knowing the last stage on which this powerful frame is fated to figure, at the same time, that I am conscious it will raise the tender feelings of the boys of the fancy, to know that that arm, the object of their highest admiration, and the terror of England, is subject to scoffs, and flung ingloriously into a filthy sink.

During a meeting held the next evening to consider the erection of a suitable memorial above the tomb, 'A gentleman present wished to know if there was any truth in the rumour of the disinterment of the body, but was assured in the most positive terms, that the sacred depository had not been violated.'

Despite this assurance a grizzly relic said to be the right arm of Donnelly is still to be seen at a pub in Kilcullen, close to the Curragh, the scene of Dan's much publicised victory over George Cooper:

> And in a glass case on the wall
> You'll see it hanging there
> The arm of Bold Dan Donnelly
> Who fought upon Kildare!

What happened to the remainder of Bold Dan will, perhaps, never be known.

The Irish poor of the time needed a national hero and the amount of stories, legends and ballyhoo surrounding the name of Donnelly equals that which sixty years later was to be attached to that other larger than life son of Erin, John L. Sullivan.

Perhaps the most famous of the Donnelly stories was the one spread by fellow-Irishman Pierce Egan that Dan had been knighted by the Prince Regent. This nonsense was swallowed by many members of the 'fancy' and has subsequently been published as fact in several boxing histories.

Egan's Celtic fabrications afforded much amusement to Professor John Wilson, the editor of *Blackwoods Magazine*, who following Donnelly's death published twenty pages of 'solemn dirges – letters of condolence – lamentations – plaintive ballads – odes – songs – an eloquent philosophical oration – wound up by an advertisement to collect expenses for a suitable memorial to be erected to the memory of Ireland's late Champion'.

Among the pages of Latin, Greek and Hebrew are verses purporting to be the productions of the leading poets of the age, including Mr WW [Wordsworth], whilst from B[yron] in Venice came verses entitled 'Child Daniel'. In allusion to the unsavoury nature of Donnelly's demise, Wilson inserts a poem containing the following lines:

> Oh, hadst thou been felled by Tom Cribb in the ring,
> Or by Carter been milled to a jelly,
> Oh, sure that would have been a more dignified thing
> Than to kick for a pain in your belly.

> A curse on the belly that robbed us of thee
> And the bowels unfit for their office;
> A curse on the poteen you swallowed so free,
> For a stomach complaint, all the doctors agree,
> Far worse than a headache or cough is.

The whole production was a witty and good-natured dig by Wilson at the pretended erudition displayed by Egan within the pages of *Boxiana*.

Egan, of course, entered wholeheartedly into the fun and reprinted several of the best poems with his own tongue-in-cheek criticism: '. . . although we do not understand the gist of them, it is no reason that many other persons connected with the prize ring should not. We feel a great loss in not having Bob Gregson at our elbow just now, for a tiny bit of his assistance . . . [Bob was considered a bit of a poet] Respecting the Latin, we unfortunately stand in a relative situation with the village school-mistress, to "skip and go on".' He continues by suggesting that Bill Gibbons and Daniel Mendoza might respectively render some assistance with the Greek [St Giles' slang] and the Hebrew.

Meanwhile back in Bully's Acre an imposing monument was raised to Sir Dan's memory. The tomb, which was wrecked within a few years of completion, displayed an epitaph chiefly remarkable as an acrostic [i.e. the initial letter of each line spelled the departed hero's name when read downwards]:

This monument, once to be seen on the Curragh of Kildare, places Donnelly's birthdate eighteen years too early. In fact, he never attained the forty-five years suggested by the inscription.

Dan rests beneath, still hold his memory dear,
Around his tomb let fall the pitying tear;
Now mingled with his kindred dust he lies;
In silence sleepeth – never more to rise
Except on that fateful day when all,
Living and dead, shall hear the trumpets call.

Death, Tyrant Death, that fell relentless foe,
Our champion levell'd, by a mortal blow;
None else, in single combat, could him harm,
No human foe resist his mighty arm.
Erin lament; bear in record his name;
Lament the man who fought to crown your fame,
Laid prostrate Cooper, Oliver and Hall,
Yielding to none, but Death, who conquers all.

Less respectful, though far more apt are Wilson's lines, reprinted in black letter by Egan:

Underneath this pillar high
Lies Sir Daniel Donnelly;

He was a stout and handy man,
And people called him "Buffing Dan;"
Knighthood he took from George's sword,
And well he wore it, by my word!
He died at last from forty-seven
Tumblers of punch he drank one even;
O'erthrown by punch, unharmed by fist,
He died unbeaten pugilist!
Such a buffer as Donnelly,
Ireland never again will see.

A story of appalling domestic tragedy surrounds the tomb at Hucknall in Nottinghamshire, which records the deaths of Ben Caunt and his wife Martha. Also inscribed on the tomb are the names of their children, Martha, aged eight, and Cornelius, six, who were burned to death in 1851 at Ben's public house, The Coach and Horses in St Martin's Lane, London. It seems likely that neither parent ever really recovered from the terrible shock; Ben died in 1861, his wife two years earlier.

Later in the century, the tomb was to attract more visitors than that of boxer-poet Lord Byron, who lies a few yards away within the church. But as early as the 1930s letters began to appear in the local press deploring the derelict condition into which the monument had been allowed to fall. Four slate plaques engraved with epitaphs were falling from their sandstone plinth and the plinth itself had subsided and was fast crumbling away. The situation became worse during the Second World War when the protective iron railings were removed for more urgent use.

At the centenary of Ben's death restoration was much discussed, but nothing actually done. Finally in 1985, after more than half a century of neglect, the inscribed plaques were fixed back in position on a reconditioned plinth, and the short tragic lives of the fighter and his family are once again commemorated in their native town.

One fighter who managed, against all the odds, not to die young was Caunt's bitter rival, William Thompson, better known as Bendigo, the pride of Nottingham.

Bendy's behaviour both in and out of the ring had always been, to say the least, eccentric and he possessed an inordinate fondness for acrobatic tricks. A broken knee-cap, which permanently shortened his right leg, and a serious head injury bore witness 'that his talent for knocking a man about extended to his own person'.

Bendigo had been sent to the house of correction on numerous occasions, both during and after his ring career. These periods of incarceration occurred mainly as a result of his association with a notorious gang of ruffians known as the 'Nottingham Lambs', who were inclined to make their presence felt at prize-fights, local elections and other social gatherings.

According to one of many alleged biographies, it was during the twenty-eighth of his sojourns in prison that he discovered God and became converted to the Revivalist sect of the Christian Religion. Upon his release Bendy took to wearing the dress of a dissenting preacher. According to Conan Doyle:

The epitaph on 'Bendigo's' rather forlorn tomb at Sneinton, Nottingham, is short and to the point, but whether or not the shifty boxer's tumbledown style of fighting actually resembled that of a lion, must remain a matter of opinion.

> His hat was like a funeral, he'd got a waiter's coat,
> With a hallelujah collar and a choker round his throat.

He became a popular speaker at various working men's missions up and down the country, and remained devoutly religious, with only occasional lapses, up until his sudden demise in the sixty-ninth year of his life at his home in Beeston, a western suburb of Nottingham. The cause of death was reputed to have been not entirely unconnected with a flight of stairs and a somersault!

Bendigo's funeral took place at St Mary's Cemetery in Nottingham, but not until strong local opposition to his being buried anywhere other than in his native Beeston had been overcome. Eventually his body had to be taken from the house under cover of darkness.

The procession to the cemetery was attended not only by large crowds composed of the rowdy element already familiar to us, but also contained the contrasting ingredient of Bendigo's many evangelical friends. The great Revivalist preacher

Richard Weaver headed the cortège, the stragglers of which paused at a public house *en route* for refreshment, which may or may not account for the following circumstance:

> . . . an elderly, clerical-looking gentleman, who had been making himself conspicuous by waving aloft an umbrella and harranguing groups of men and women, caused himself to be unceremoniously removed from the spot by knocking off the speaker's headgear . . . He had evidently been bibulating too freely, and therefore was given the attention of several constables.

The sculptural monument subsequently erected over the grave is one of a handful of rather desolate tombs remaining in what has become a 'Garden of Rest'. The memorial is surmounted by a carved stone lion, a smaller version of that which adorns the tomb of John Jackson at Brompton. Bendy's animal holds a scroll displaying his date of death, 'Augt. 23RD 1880', whilst on the plinth below are inscribed the lines:

> In life always brave, fighting like a Lion,
> In death like a lamb, tranquil in Zion.

To which might well be appended the words of that earlier and most famous of converts to the ways of righteousness: 'I have fought a good fight, I have finished my course.'

SUGGESTED FURTHER READING

Apart from the six rare volumes of *Boxiana*, published from 1812 to 1829, and the three of *Pugilistica*, last published in 1906, most of the works referred to in the foregoing pages are readily available in modern editions.

A facsimile of the first volume of *Boxiana* was produced by Vance Harvey Publishing in 1971, and a selection, mainly from the first volume, was edited by John Ford and published by The Folio Society in 1976.

I have found the following titles particularly useful with regard to the general history of pugilism:

Andre, Sam. and Fleischer, Nat. *A Pictorial History of Boxing*, Hamlyn, 1976.

Batchelor, Denzil. *The Boxing Companion*, Eyre & Spottiswoode, 1964.

In addition, the heyday of the prize-ring is comprehensively dealt with in:

Ford, John. *Prizefighting: The Age of Regency Boximania*, David & Charles, 1971.

Reid, J. C. *Bucks and Bruisers: Pierce Egan and Regency England*, Routledge & Kegan Paul, 1971.

Among the many other books consulted, various aspects of the art, literature and background of the subject may be found in the following short selection:

Burke, Joseph and Caldwell, Colin. *Hogarth, The Complete Engravings*, Thames & Hudson, 1968.

Chesney, Kellow. *The Victorian Underworld*, Penguin, 1972.

Cieszkowski, Krzystof. 'Bendigo the Boxer', article in History Today, 1984.

Curl, James Stevens. *The Victorian Celebration of Death*, David & Charles, 1972.

Finley, M. I. and Pleket, H. W. *The Olympic Games – The First Thousand Years*, Chatto & Windus, 1976.

George, M. Dorothy. *Hogarth to Cruikshank: Social change in Graphic Satire*, Allen Lane The Penguin Press, 1967.

Goldman, Paul. *Sporting Life: An Anthology of British Sporting Prints*, British Museum Publications, 1983.

Lloyd, Alan. *The Great Prize Fight*, Cassell, 1977.

Lynch, Bohun. *The Prize Ring*, Country Life, 1925.

Magriel, Paul (ed). *Memoirs of the life of Daniel Mendoza*, Batsford, 1951. (First published 1816).

Malcolmson, Robert W. *Popular recreations in English Society*, Cambridge, 1973.

Mandell, Richard D. *Sport: A Cultural History*, Columbia University Press, 1984.

Marchard, Leslie A. (ed). *Byron's Letters and Journals* (eleven volumes), John Murray, 1973–81.

Myler, Patrick. *Regency Rogue; Dan Donnelly, his life and legends*, The O'Brien Press, 1976.

Nicholson, Renton. *Rogue's Progress: The Autobiography of 'Lord Chief Baron' Nicholson*, Longmans, 1966. (First published *c*.1860).

Partridge, Eric. *The Penguin Dictionary of Historical Slang* (abridged by J. Simpson), Penguin, 1972.

Paulson, Ronald. *The Art of Hogarth*, Phaidon, 1975.

Reynolds, John Hamilton. *The Fancy*, Garland, 1977. (First published 1820).

Wilder, F. L. *English Sporting Prints*, Thames & Hudson, 1974.

Young, G. M. (ed). *Early Victorian England*, Oxford, 1971.

British Sporting Painting 1650–1850, (exhibition catalogue), Arts Council of Great Britain, 1974.

Career details of most of the leading pugilists are to be found in the *Dictionary of National Biography*, while issues of *Bell's Life in London* may be consulted at the British Newspaper Library, Colindale.

By the time that Gustave Doré drew this boxing booth at the Derby in the 1870s, boxing gloves had largely superseded bare knuckles.

INDEX

Note: Works of fiction and fictitious characters are not usually indexed separately, but are included under the appropriate author (i.e. Dickens' novel *Dombey and Son* together with his pugilistic character 'The Game Chicken', will be found within: Dickens, Charles).

Page numbers set in *Italics* refer to illustrations.